I0529122

Moonfish
PRESS

GIORGIO & MARIA

SPEAK THEIR NAMES

Janet Dunn, Nancy Tennant,
Linda Tennant, and Diane Rudash

Moonfish
PRESS

Copyright © 2025 by Dunn, Tennant, Tennant, and Rudash.
All Rights Reserved
Published by Moonfish Press

No part of this publication may be reproduced, stored in a retrieval
system, or transmitted in any form or by any means, electronic,
mechanical, photocopying, recording, scanning, or otherwise, except
by permission under Section 108 of the 1976 United States Copyright
Act, without either prior written consent of the publisher or
authorization through payment of the appropriate fee. Requests to the
publisher for permission should be addressed to
dr.nancytennant@gmail.com.

Readers should be aware that internet sites offered as citations or
sources for further information may have changed or disappeared
between when this was written and when it was read.

Disclosure: No endorsements or financial associations exist between
the author and suggested websites, authors, or references.

Limit of Liability/Disclaimer of Warranty: While the publisher and
authors have used their best efforts to prepare the book, they make no
representations or warranties regarding the accuracy or completeness of
`merchantability or fitness for a particular purpose.

Citations: Every effort was made to cite key sources, but due to the
nature of the prose, citations are limited.

Library of Congress Cataloging-in-Publication Data

Dunn, Tennant, Tennant, & Rudash

ISBN: 979-8-9916150-3-7 (Paperback)
Library of Congress Control Number: 2024920151

First Edition: May 2025

To our beloved families,

past, present, and future.

TABLE OF CONTENTS

FOREWORD

My Raspa/Simonetti family began immigrating to America around 1903. The first was Aunt Rosalie Raspa (Gelfo), who settled in Rivesville, West Virginia, lured there by the thriving coal industry. Rivesville is in north central West Virginia along Route 19, between Fairmont and Morgantown along the Monongahela River. Rivesville was a segregated town divided into three subdivisions. Native-born West Virginians lived primarily in a section called Highlawns. The Hites, named after a local coal mine owner, was a residential part of town where immigrants lived. Greentown was unique in that it was both residential (and home to immigrants) and commercial. Greentown got its name because the houses were all painted green and owned by the coal company.

Rivesville had numerous coal mines, as well as a company store and a medical clinic linked to the mining operations. The miners received their wages in "company scrip," which they had to redeem for food, gasoline, and other essential goods at the company store. Rivesville was also home to a large power plant owned by the Monongahela Power Company, which supplied electricity to the region. A main railroad line ran along the river through Greentown, facilitating access to the coal mines.

Our family lived in Greentown and owned businesses. My uncles Frank and Ralph Raspa owned the State Theater; my father, Giorgio (George), owned a shoe shop; one aunt and uncle owned a grocery store; and another uncle owned a beer garden.

As the youngest and only surviving child of Giorgio and Maria Simonetti, I feel compelled to share some reflections on my parents. My mother was a truly caring person. She and my father were very social, surrounded by many friends and acquaintances. My mother had numerous female friends (*commares*). She could read and write in Italian, while many of her friends were illiterate in English and Italian. She assisted them in drafting letters in Italian to send to their relatives in Italy. Although my mother never learned to speak English, she understood it. As a child, I communicated with her solely in Italian. This ability proved beneficial later in my adult life. While pursuing my doctorate at Brandeis University, I was required to pass a language exam to earn my degree. When asked if I was fluent in any other language, I explained that I was fluent in Italian but could not read it. My adviser arranged for me to be tutored in reading Italian. My exam involved translating a social policy article from Italian to English. With my tutor's guidance, I successfully passed the exam.

My mother was kindhearted and always helped others. In the early 1940s, an impoverished handyman regularly did yard work at our home. My mother made sure to feed and take care of him. She was kind to everyone and knew what it was like to be overlooked. Additionally, she was an artisan who could sew and crochet beautifully.

My father was very sociable, gregarious, and well-liked by everyone. He had many friends in the local area and other parts of the state. He was a member of the Christopher Columbus Lodge in Fairmont, an Italian American association. He loved singing, dancing, and socializing at the lodge on Sunday afternoons. Each week, when he came home from the lodge, he would ride with different friends and occasionally invite them into the house for food. He would wake my mother to prepare a meal even if she was already in bed for the night. My mother was well-known among their friends in town for being quite the cook.

My father was kind and loving. I remember him playing Santa at Christmas. A coal-burning stove heated our home since we didn't have a fireplace. During Christmas, he filled one of my mother's cotton stockings with money, fruit, and candy from Santa and hung it on the stove for me. My father also loved the opera. When the Metropolitan Opera was in season on Saturdays, he would close the shop early, come home, and we would listen to operas together on the radio. Despite the many trials our family faced, I had a wonderful childhood.

Anita

Anita S. Harbert

Note: The images of fingerprints used throughout are for artistic purposes only. Public domain.

INTRODUCTION

The first generation of immigrants wants to survive, the second wants to assimilate, and the third wants to remember.

M. L. Hansen

In 2023, Anita Harbert, Giorgio and Maria's youngest and last living child, had an idea: to create a book about her Simonetti/Raspa family to honor her parents. The book would encompass stories about her ancestors, siblings, and children. Anita wanted to share the tales of her childhood within the Simonetti/Raspa family, including the journeys, hardships, dreams, funny stories, and love that shaped their lives. The book's central focus would be Giorgio and Maria (Raspa) Simonetti, known to their grandchildren as Poppy and Nonna, and the lives they built for themselves and their children—Thresia, Carmella, Ralphine, Frank, and Anita—after immigrating to the United States in 1920/1921.

Writing biographies can be complex. They capture only fragments of a person's life. Memories, stories, pictures, records, and other mementos are used to piece together individuals' lives, often long after those individuals have passed. This task can be challenging, especially if the subjects died long ago and the trail, in some respects, has gone cold. Such circumstances often leave gaps that may never be filled. As time progresses and the world changes, personal artifacts are lost and photographs and memories fade. Anita aimed to capture and preserve, as much as possible, the narrative of Giorgio and Maria's life and the interconnected lives that spun from their epicenter.

The four Tennant sisters, Anita's nieces—Janet, Nancy, Linda, and Diane—took up the challenge to write the biography. We were aided by our aunt Carol and many cousins and cousins-in-law. While we approached the project with eyes wide open, we had no idea that we would undertake a search and rescue mission before we could write the biography. We discovered, cataloged, and archived numerous artifacts as we carefully pored over everything we could find in order to recount Giorgio and Maria's stories. The artifacts included genealogy databases, photos, letters, and stories told by living relatives, and memories, to name a few. We digitized these resources and cataloged and stored all physical resources—photos, letters, etc.—in one central place.

We relentlessly searched for old pictures, scouring every possible lead. To illustrate the thoroughness of our search, one effort focused on a single image we recalled from our youth that was now missing. It became the driving force behind our need to recreate the story of Giorgio and Maria's lives, enhanced by the most intriguing visuals. We sought a photo of a young Giorgio and Maria standing in front of a large garage-style rolling door with horizontal metal slats. We believe this picture was taken in Italy. If that's true, it's our only photo of them in Italy.

We looked everywhere for the picture. We remembered it on our mother's (Ralphine's) drop leaf table in her living room, mounted in a small oval frame. We asked every family member if they remembered the picture and had a copy, but no one did. Some knew of the picture; others did not remember it. Eventually, our cousin Rosemary remembered the picture and believed she had a copy in her basement. Unfortunately, the area where the picture was stored had been turned into a storage space and she couldn't access it. She did everything short of bodysurfing to the picture's location on the family room's far wall, but it was not to be. After a long search, we finally found the picture in the depths of Janet's files.

The picture was dear to us before, but now it was even more so after our search-and-rescue mission, so we decided to put a version of it on the book's cover. Once we had it in hand again, we examined it more closely, using Ken Burns's style and taking in every detail that might suggest its backstory.

Fifty years after first seeing it, it is a testament to a great love. The picture is amazing to take in after all that has transpired. The young Giorgio and Maria are positioned close to each other, closer than the customs of Italy at the time would permit a young single man and woman to be. Maria is sitting, and Giorgio is standing to her left. Maria is young, maybe nineteen. Her long dark hair is parted on the side and pulled back over her ears. She is looking directly into the camera; her lips are closed, and she is not smiling. If you look only at the lower half of her face, you might think she looks stern. But when you look at her eyes, something magical happens. The focal point of her dark, shining eyes makes her beautiful young face look happy, relaxed, and in love. She is wearing a dark coat with a single button at the waist, and no doubt the clothing peaking from underneath is her best. Around her neck hangs a pearl choker. She is wearing earrings, but the quality of the picture makes it impossible to see them. It also looks like she has a ring on the middle finger of her left hand, which is resting on her thigh. The cropped picture leaves out her right side, so we can't tell if she has more jewelry on her other hand.

When you first look at the picture, your eyes go directly to Giorgio. His charismatic face and stylish clothes suggest a young man focused on how he presents himself to the world. His oversized wool newsboy cap is perfectly positioned, the curve of the bill expertly framing Giorgio's forehead. His face is round and handsome, with kind and inquisitive brown eyes. He looks like a man of means who is in control of his destiny. His dress is dapper, contrasting black and gray, and punctuated with a crisp white shirt. His shirt features a starched collar with a collar stay underneath to keep the collar points and his tie in place. There is a pin on the black tie in the middle of his chest, the nature of which is challenging to make out; it looks gold. His tie is fashioned into a perfect half-Windsor-type knot. Smart. What is striking about his attire is the perfectly fitted vest, which is light in color, featuring a watch pocket on the side. His black jacket, again perfectly fitted, has a white pocket handkerchief. The cuffs of his white shirt peek out about a half inch below each sleeve. We can't see if he has on cufflinks, but given the style of his dress, they would surely be included. He is wearing black pants. A remarkable feature of his attire is the long, draped gold watch chain below his vest. His left hand is casually in his pocket, adding informality to his look.

What makes the picture so extraordinary is his right hand comfortably perched on Maria's left shoulder. This implies an intimacy rarely seen in photos of this era, especially without a chaperone! They are closely intertwined, displaying great comfort with each other. His right hand and arm, in the center of the image, are comfortably perched on Maria's left shoulder. Giorgio's hand is relaxed, strong, and skilled, almost in contrast to his gentlemanly and refined attire. It's an incredible picture.

We don't know where the picture was taken or for what purpose. In our desire to tell the story and fill in what we don't know, we assume it was taken in Italy. Italy is filled with the type of metal rolling doors shown in the picture; shopkeepers and many homes use them to protect their doors and windows from thieves. We also assume it is an engagement or wedding photo. However, we have no evidence that they were married in Italy before leaving to go to the United States in December 1920 as part of the great emigration from Southern Italy to the United States.

This single picture and the quest to find it symbolize our dedication and love for our work. We sifted through over five hundred artifacts over two years of research and writing. To complicate the genealogy challenge, many of the letters and documents we uncovered were in Italian, a language none of us speak. This forced us to depend on translators, translation apps, and AI (artificial intelligence). However, there's always uncertainty about whether you have captured the full nuances and quirks of the original text when you don't speak the language. Moreover, the Italian dialect in many artifacts is no longer spoken in Italy. The language barrier and the involvement of different countries made our genealogy research even more challenging. At times, the obstacles seemed insurmountable. Yet, our tenacity, or, as some might say, stubbornness, prevailed.

Anita was right: we need to tell the story. It's a remarkable one that spans two continents and includes Giorgio's Italian military service in WWI, his apprenticeship and work as a shoemaker for the Municipal Theater in Catanzaro, or Il Teatro Comunale di Catanzaro (and what our family calls the Opera House), Giorgio and Maria's journey by ship to immigrate to the United States, and their challenging life in a coal mining community in West Virginia. Giorgio's professional arc swiftly transitioned from making shoes for sopranos and tenors to crafting boots for coal miners. The latter part of the narrative includes Giorgio's tragic and untimely death, the growth and success of the remaining family, the diaspora of Rivesville with all its small-town intrigue, and the generations of children and grandchildren who grew up and carved out their own paths. While this story concludes in the mid-1970s with Maria's passing, what Giorgio and Maria started lives on in subsequent generations. Throughout it all, laughter, unity, and love created enduring bonds among sisters, brothers, cousins, and second cousins, all beginning with a dream of coming to America—where, at least in decades past, you could forge your future.

When do we actually die? Is it our medical death when all bodily functions cease, or is it something else that signals death? According to Hemingway, it may depend on those who remain:

Every man has two deaths, when he is buried in the ground, and the last time someone says his name. In some ways, men (sic) can be immortal.[1]

With this book, we hope that Giorgio and Maria will be remembered across generations and become *immortal* in some small way. Their story lives on in each of their descendants, as does their DNA of survival, love, family, and hard work.

* * *

There's only one thing left to do:

Speak Their Names / Dite i Loro Nomi

---

[1] This quote is commonly attributed (but unverified) to Ernest Hemingway, but it has been popularized in a slightly different form in the 2017 documentary *Mission Control: The Unsung Heroes of Apollo* directed by David Fairhead.

CHAPTER 1: WHY LEAVE?

Overcoming poverty is not a gesture of charity. It is an act of justice. It is the protection of a fundamental human right, the right to dignity and a decent life.

Nelson Mandela

It is hard to be a century and continent away and understand why people would leave their homeland. To grasp this, we need context. What was it like to emigrate in the first two decades of the twentieth century? We must share a story about politics, geography, economies, taxes, natural disasters, and oppression to comprehend.

Politics, Economies, Taxes & Natural Disasters

The region's beauty is overwhelming when traveling through Catanzaro in Southern Italy. This majestic beauty includes the northern Sila Mountains and the southern Serre Calabresi Mountains, the glistening waters of the Ionian Sea, and the charming mountainside roads and towns that roll up and down the hillsides of Catanzaro. However, over a century ago, the region was drastically different. In large numbers, southern Italian families left their homeland to emigrate to the United States. In 1920, among those who departed was Giorgio Simonetti, a twenty-six-year-old sophisticated tradesman and military veteran from the town of Stilo, along with his wife or fiancée, Maria Raspa, a twenty-three-year-old young woman from Petilia Policastro.

In the 1860s, Italy was a fragmented region marked by military invasions and peasant uprisings. Giorgio and Maria's parents and grandparents likely lived through this national turmoil and unrest. Eventually, the country unified and emerged as the Kingdom of Italy, facing significant economic disparities between the North and South. The North severely neglected Calabria, viewing the southern region as backward and impoverished. With the powerful in control, the powerless were at their mercy. Due to a lack of government investment in education, approximately 70 percent of Southerners were illiterate. The government feared that an educated population would demand changes and pose a threat to the elite's power.

Unification and the King of Italy

The formation of the modern Italian state began in 1861 with the unification of most of the peninsula under the House of Savoy (Piedmont-Sardinia) into the Kingdom of Italy. By 1871, Italy incorporated Venetia and the former Papal States (including Rome) following the Franco-Prussian War (1870–71). Unification made the southern part of Italy poorer, mainly because the House of Savoy did very little to assist the South in its development.

King of Italy Portrait. Library of Congress, loc.getarchive.net, [date unknown]. Public domain.

Many Southern Italians did not respect the Italian government, as it failed to lift the South out of its poverty. Meanwhile, many remained loyal to the Roman Catholic Church, but the Church prohibited poor Catholic men from voting in elections, allowing only landowning aristocrats to gain political power. This poor relationship with the Church was disastrous for the Italian government, weakening the state and enabling organized crime groups like the Mafia to form a "parallel state" that coexisted alongside the corrupt Italian government.

Victor Emmanuel III ruled the Kingdom of Italy from July 29, 1900, to May 9, 1946. As a hesitant and indecisive ruler, Victor Emmanuel's reign was marked by political violence and instability. His inaction allowed Italian Fascism to rise.

Fast-forward a few decades, long after Giorgio and Maria left Italy. The king's support for Benito Mussolini tarnished the image of the Italian monarchy to the point that it was eventually abolished. He was content to let Mussolini govern Italy, viewing Il Duce as a strong man who spared him the trouble of dealing with various politicians as he had needed to do before Mussolini rose to power in November 1921.

Within a year of the end of WWII, public opinion compelled a referendum on whether to keep the monarchy or establish a republic. Hoping to support the monarchist cause, Victor Emmanuel formally abdicated in favor of his son, who took the throne as Umberto II on May 9, 1946. The Italian conductor Toscanini declared that he would not return to Italy as a subject of the "degenerate king" and, more broadly, if the House of Savoy was governing. Ultimately, the

1

monarchy was abolished, and Victor Emmanuel and the other members of the House of Savoy were required to leave the country.

The Start of the Great Migration

Of the four million Italians who came to the United States between 1890 and 1920, around 80 percent were from Southern Italy. Most men worked as peasant farmers, fishermen, and shoemakers, and both men and women worked as tradespeople. These peasants often referred to Southern Italy as the land of *la miseria.*

Southern Italy was plagued by a combination of life-altering economic and natural catastrophes. These disasters significantly influenced the decisions of Italian immigrants. In the 1870s, the Italian government forced Southern peasants to pay exorbitant taxes on diseased vineyards. To raise revenue in the late 1870s, the government imposed excessive taxes on wheat (which had already dropped to record low prices) and salt used as a food preservative. This caused financial strain for peasant farmers. In northern Calabria, farmers' crops were often wiped out due to disease. Wealthy absentee landowners expected the peasants to absorb the costs of these losses.

1

Map of Southern Italy.https://picryl.com/media/1814-thomson-map-of-southern-italy-naples-sicily-geographicus-naplessicily-b94c66 [date unknown]. Public domain.

Bread riots erupted in 1881 when the region faced a lack of work and food. In 1882, a cholera epidemic ravaged the area. Over twenty-one thousand Italians died from malaria as late as 1887. The citrus crops suffered several poor harvests due to drought and diseased trees. This allowed the United States citrus industry to gain an advantage in the world fruit market in the 1890s.

Similar drought conditions destroyed vineyards, enabling the French wine industry to infringe on the Italian wine industry. In 1910, the eruption of Mount Etna in Sicily killed ten thousand people. Sandwiched between these events, Southern Italians experienced a litany of miseries.

The crushing taxes imposed on residents were especially debilitating for Southern Italians. By the end of the nineteenth century, Italy had the highest taxes in Europe, placing a heavy burden on those least able to pay. Excise taxes were applied to essential items like salt, sugar, tobacco, liquor, flour, bread, macaroni, and other government-controlled goods. The central government taxed heavily, and the provinces followed suit. Some estimates indicate an overall tax rate of 30 percent, which was quite high compared to France (12 percent), Germany (8 percent), and England (6 percent). This heavy tax burden on the South contributed to the region's bankruptcy, yet what Southern Italians resented most were the Northern Italians who held influential positions in Rome and affected the lives of the Southern Italians.

1

Messina Earthquake 1908. https://picryl.com/search?q=Richard%20El-lis%202730%2C%20Messina%20earthquake%201908.]. Public domain.

In 1905, a series of earthquakes rocked Calabria, resulting in the deaths of as many as thirty thousand people. In 1906, Mount Vesuvius erupted, burying entire towns near Naples. On December 28, 1908, a 7.1 magnitude earthquake struck the town of Messina, about one hundred miles west of Constanza, killing approximately eighty-two thousand people. Towns were demolished, and 293 aftershocks occurred between December 1908 and January 1909. Giorgio would have been fourteen years old, and Maria would have been eleven. An Italian essay described the harsh conditions in Southern Italy.

> *In rural hilltop villages like Roggiano Gravina, entire families lived in single-room, cell-like structures where barnyard animals often slept. Peasants were typically short in stature and malnourished. Their diet largely consisted of bread and oil, perhaps some wild greens, with meat rarely eaten. In the mornings, workers filed into the fields and valleys below to toil under oppressive heat, using primitive agricultural tools and methods of tilling soil in land pockmarked with malarial water.*[2]

1

Three Calabrian Cities

A trio of southern Italian cities in Calabria serves as characters in the story of Giorgio and Maria. They are Stilo, where Giorgio was born; Petilia Policastro, where Maria was born; and Catanzaro, where they almost certainly met, fell in love, and planned their emigration to America. All three cities are in Calabria, at the toe and instep of the boot of Italy. The climate of all three is typically Mediterranean: temperate and characterized by a windy spring and autumn. All three cities are high in the mountains, averaging fourteen thousand feet above the Ionian Sea.

PETILIA POLICASTRO

CATANZARO

STILO

[2]Rotondaro, "Which Italian America?"

Stilo

The village of Stilo is nestled on the picturesque slopes of Mount Consolino. The undisputed symbol of Stilo is the Byzantine church La Cattolica, one of Calabria's most renowned churches. It was built between the tenth and eleventh centuries by Basilian monks, who initially settled in caves hewn from the rock in the surrounding mountains and carved out rooms and rock churches, leaving behind impressive frescoes. Stilo overlooks the olive- and vine-covered hills and offers stunning views of the Ionian Sea.

Stilo is eighty-one miles south of Petilia Policastro in the Reggio Calabria region. The city's foliage is not green and lush like the tropics; it consists of cacti and other succulents and has an arid feel. Stilo's economy is primarily agricultural, producing cereals, oil, wine, and cheese. Iron and lead mines are nearby. Today, the population is 2,300.

1

Stilo, La Cattolica, photo taken by authors, 2016.

Petilia Policastro

Petilia Policastro is in the province of Crotone, in Calabria, Italy. According to Greek mythology, the city of Petilia was founded by Philoctetes, the archer famous for killing Paris in the Trojan War. The town was home to Pope Anterus during the third century. In the historic center, in front of the current façade of the Church of San Nicola Pontefice, is a cemetery with rock tombs cut from the stone from the surrounding mountains. The town relies on producing olive oil, wine, cereals, citrus fruit, and breeding cattle.

Today, roughly five thousand people live in the city. When we visited the town in 2016, it still had a small-town feel. In fact, on the way to the town, our car had to pull over and cede the right of way to a herd of longhorn cattle and their *butteri*, or Italian cowboys, who were passing.

1

Arial view of Petilia Policastro.

Catanzaro

Contemporary view of Catanzaro, Italy.

If you were trying to pinpoint a location on the map directly between Petilia Policastro and Stilo, you couldn't get much closer than Catanzaro, with both cities approximately forty-two miles from Catanzaro's center. Catanzaro is the largest city and regarded as the capital of Calabria. Catanzaro means "the city of two seas" because it lies at Italy's narrowest point, nestled between the Ionian and Tyrrhenian seas. Today it is home to around eighty-six thousand residents and has an urban sensibility. When you include the surrounding municipalities, it has nearly two hundred thousand inhabitants. It is known as the city of the three V's, VVV, which highlight three significant features of the city: Saint Vitalian, the patron saint of Catanzaro; velvet, due to the town's historical importance as a textile hub; and wind (*vento* in Italian), which brings the strong breezes from the Ionian Sea and the La Sila mountain range. Currently, Catanzaro's economy is primarily driven by the tertiary services sector. The industries mainly consist of medium- and small-sized companies operating within a local market.

Southern Italians left to pursue better lives in the United States for many reasons, including politics, economies, taxes, natural disasters, and oppression. This background of life in Southern Italy at the turn of the twentieth century begins our story of Giorgio and Maria.

* * *

They were growing up and coming of age in a world about to come undone.

Italian Roots

Where am I from?
What did they do?
Where did they live?
Tell the story about you.

Teach me all about
the things that used to be.
Where can I find this
on my family tree.

Answer the questions.
Fill the blank spaces.
Help me put an image
to all those past faces.

Where are they buried?
How did they die?
What purpose did they serve
when they were alive?

I feel it's important
to find what made me.
The mannerisms, the looks,
the behaviors you see.

So, help me put together
all the pieces, finally.
So I can complete the story
of this amazing dynasty.

CHAPTER 2: SUSPENDED INNOCENCE
1900–1914

The greatest adventure is what lies ahead.

J. R. R. Tolkien

At the turn of the century, Southern Italy was a rural collection of villages with a warm, temperate Mediterranean climate. The region shares the beautiful dichotomy of mountains and beaches, making it stunningly beautiful. It is wedged between the Ionian and Tyrrhenian Seas, with the Strait of Messina separating it from Sicily. Ancient Greeks settled it, and the Byzantines introduced silk-making to Calabria, making it a central hub for European luxury textiles. In the south of the region is Stilo, where Giorgio was born.

Giorgio's Family in Stilo

Giorgio's parents were Dominico Carmelo Simonetti and Teresa De-Luca. Dominico was born in 1854 in Mongiana, in the province of Vibo Valentia, about thirty-one miles southwest of Catanzaro. We have a record of Dominico's mother, Rosaria Simonetta (spelled with an "a"), who was born in 1831 and died in 1878. Unfortunately, we do not have any information about Dominico's father. Teresa DeLuca, Giorgio's mother, was born in 1860 in Stilo. We found a record of Teresa's mother, Vittoria DeLuca, who was born in 1822, but we don't have a date of death for her. We also lack any information on Teresa's father.

We don't know how or why Dominico got to Stilo. We know very little about them. Their marriage certificate shows they married in Stilo on September 16, 1882. Our records of the Simonetti family in Italy before and following 1900 are scarce and sketchy, but they show that Dominico and Teresa had seven children.

b. 1897	b. 1894	b. 1891	b. 1888	b. 1886	b. 1884	unknown
Giovanni Francesco	Giorgio Vincenzo	Maria Francesca	Maria Luisa	Francesco Vincenzo	Rosaria Maria Francesca	Lisa

To the left, standing, is Lisa. We know this from an oral history shared by Italian relatives who presented this picture to American relatives during a visit to Italy in the 1970s. The little girl clutching the doll is Lisa's daughter, Maria. Dominico Carmello Simonetti, Giorgio's father, sits in the chair while his mother, Teresa DeLuca, stands beside him. The date of the picture is unknown, although we speculate that Teresa, appearing to be around forty, suggests the photo was taken in the early 1890s. Family archives.

The earliest photo we have of Giorgio. We think the photo was taken when he was two years old in 1896. Family archives.

We found this extremely damaged photo of Giorgio's family, which raises more questions than answers. We believe the picture was taken around 1901, after the previous picture that included Lisa, Dominico, Teresa, and the little girl, Maria. We assume that Dominico has passed away, which is the best explanation for why he is not in the photo. We also suspect that their youngest son, Giovanni, may not have survived, which explains his absence. Additionally, we are unsure why Lisa is not present in the image. We do not know who the siblings are in the back row, but our best guesses are (L–R): Rosaria, Maria Luisa (whose face was badly damaged in the photo), Francesco, and Maria Francesca. However, our degree of certainty is low.

We feel more certain about the front row (L–R): Giorgio, Teresa DeLuca. Teresa appears to be about fifty. The wild card in the picture is Giorgio. During the late nineteenth and early twentieth centuries, it was common in many parts of the world, including Southern Italy, to dress young boys in dresses or gowns. This practice was not unique to Italy; rather, it was part of a broader cultural norm across Europe and the United States at that time. In Southern Italy, there was a belief that dressing boys in dresses or more feminine clothing could protect them from evil spirits or the *malocchio* (evil eye). This superstition arose from the idea that boys should be disguised to avoid attracting the attention of malevolent forces. In both his baby picture and this photograph, where we are assuming he is about seven, Giorgio is wearing an Italian horn, also known as a *cornicello*. This amulet symbolizes good luck and offers protection against the malocchio, a curse believed to cause misfortune, injury, or harm to babies and mothers. In the birth records, "Simonetti" is sometimes spelled "Simonetta." We have Rosaria's death date, which we speculate was in 1978, although the death record is hard to read. We don't have the years when the rest of the siblings died, nor do we have a date of death for Dominico. Teresa DeLuca died in 1950. We also know that Giorgio was the only family member to come to America.

While visiting Stilo in 2016, we didn't have an address for the Simonettis. Even though we didn't know where Giorgio's childhood home was, we got a sense of the village. The view from its mountainous location down to the sea was quite stunning. Stilo lacks a city center, which is not typical of many small villages in Italy. We saw La Cattolica, also known as the Cattolica di Stilo, now a UNESCO site. This church was built in the ninth century as part of the Byzantine Empire and is one of the oldest Catholic churches in the world, showcasing an interior adorned with faint yet magnificent frescoes.

Maria's Family in Petilia Policastro

Maria Raspa was born on April 13, 1897, and grew up in the village of Petilia Policastro in the province of Crotone. Crotone is one of five provinces in the Calabria region of Southern Italy. Maria's father was Nicola Raspa and her mother was Rosa Benincasa.

While we don't have his date of birth, evidence suggests that Nicola's family was working class. The children received some education and could read and write. Nicola passed away in 1907, coinciding with the time when his children started to emigrate. We could not find very much information on Nicola's parents, but Rosa's parents were Joseph Benincasa (b. January 26, 1833) and Isabella Caruso (b. November 8, 1933). We do not have dates for either of their births or deaths. Rosa and Nicola had six children.

b. 1897	b. 1894	b. 1892	b. 1891	b. 1889	b. 1884
Maria	Raffaele	Francesco (Frank)	Rosalie	Angelina	Isabella

Anita, standing on Maria's street, Vico Pace,
in Petilia Policastro, taken by the authors. 2016.

2

We don't know much more about the Raspa siblings' childhood. In 2016, we visited Petilia Policastro to see where they lived. We do know that four of Maria's siblings and her mother, Rosa, emigrated to America.

In 1907, the same year their father passed away, the Raspa family began to emigrate to the United States. All of Maria's siblings eventually moved to the United States except for one, her sister Isabella. Isabella chose to stay in Italy and use her travel-to-America funds to educate her son, Costantino. She married Carmen Pietro Geremico, (spelling varies) who was later killed in World War I. Maria's mother, Rosa Benincasa, also emigrated. We don't have letters or stories about why the Raspas and Giorgio decided to come to West Virginia, but we do have some ideas.

In the early 1900s, coal company procurers from the United States came to Southern Italy to recruit miners. Southern Italy had sulfur, iron ore, salt, coal mines, and marble quarries, and so the area also had a rich supply of manual laborers seeking a better life. Many coal companies established recruiting offices in Calabria and promised the "Golden Door" (from Emma Lazarus' poem, "The New Colossus," inscribed on the Statue of Liberty) to all.

The Great Raspa Migration

Beginning in 1907, a steady stream of Raspas traveled westward across the Atlantic. The first person from Rosa's family who came to the United States was Dominick Foreste, Rosa Benincasa's son from her first marriage. He emigrated to Elkins, West Virginia, in 1903. Clearly, the coal mines in West Virginia had recruited him. Once Dominick was established, the floodgates for family migration opened for Maria's siblings. How fortunate they were to leave before the war began in 1914. Without a doubt, her two brothers would have been conscripted and might not have survived WWI.

In 1907, Rosalie Raspa (b. 1891) became the first sibling of the Raspa family to arrive in America. She was the third of six children born to Nicola Raspa (b. unknown, d. 1907) and Rosa Benincasa (b. 1856). Rosalie was around sixteen when she departed from the Port of Naples, Italy, on the S.S. Algeria, arriving in New York on July 22, 1907. According to the ship's "Arriving Passenger and Crew Lists," she was five feet tall with black hair, black eyes, and a brown complexion. Her birthplace is misspelled on the form. She was recorded as married, and her husband paid for her passage. The form also indicates that her husband, who was in the United States, was named Domenico Elia. Another entry reveals that Domenico Elia resided in Grafton, West Virginia. Although Rosalie's brother arranged a marriage for her in the United States, she ran off with a man named Giovanni Gelfo once she arrived, leading to the cancellation of the arranged marriage. How did a sixteen-year-old unmarried woman, the first of her siblings from a paternalistic society who had never left her village, muster the courage and determination to undertake such an extraordinary journey alone? The answer remains unknown, but it speaks volumes about her grit, spirit, and determination.

In 1910, Angelina Raspa (b. 1889) arrived in America from Naples, Italy, aboard the S.S. Batavia on June 10. She was about twenty-one at that time. According to the 1930 US census, Angelina could read and write. She married Domenico Gerarde (spelling according to the WWI registration) or Gerarda (spelling varies) in 1904. Various spellings of his name appear in different places, but we use Gearde.

Angelina was around fifteen years old when she married Domenico Gearde in Italy. Census records suggest that Domenico was roughly seven years older than Angelina. Her niece, Anita, remembers hearing stories that Angelina's mother-in-law would spank her if she believed the young bride had misbehaved, treating Angelina as someone old enough to marry but still young enough to be punished like a child. It's unclear whether Domenico Gearde was already in America when Angelina arrived, as he was not listed on the ship's manifest with her.

In 1913, brothers Francesco (Frank) Raspa (b. 1892) and Raffaele (Ralph) Raspa (b. 1894) traveled together on the S.S. San Giovanni and were among the next to arrive in America. Frank was about twenty years old and the fourth of the six children, while Ralph was around eighteen years old and the fifth of the six children. The manifest indicates that Frank and Ralph left Naples, Italy, on April 19, 1913, and arrived in New York on May 3, 1913. The manifest also lists both men as shoemakers who paid their own passage. Francesco stood at 5'3" with a natural complexion, brown hair, and brown eyes, and he carried sixty-three dollars (two thousand in today's dollars). Raffaele was 5' (likely incorrect, as other documents list him as 5'5") and had a natural complexion, brown hair, and brown eyes as well. He had twenty-five dollars (eight hundred in today's dollars). Later documents note that Raffaele is missing his right hand's first and little fingers, but no missing fingers are recorded on the ship's manifest under "marks of identification." They both listed their mother, Rosa Benincasa, as their contact in Italy and Domenico Gearde of Fairmont, West Virginia, as their destination in America.

The Artisan Shoemaker

We don't know when or why Giorgio moved to Catanzaro. We speculate he went there to become a shoemaker's (*calzolaio*) apprentice. In the early twentieth century, few good job options existed for young men and women in the region. Most men in Southern Italy were unskilled laborers, farm workers, shopkeepers, and fishermen. A handful were skilled tradesmen like carpenters, bricklayers, masons, tailors, and barbers. Many women worked as midwives, laundresses, weavers, or seamstresses. Giorgio likely became a shoemaker's apprentice in his teenage years, perhaps starting around 1910 at age sixteen.

We know that Giorgio came of age in the cultural center of Catanzaro, Il Teatro Comunale di Catanzaro, or, as our family called it, the "Opera House." Our family's understanding is that Giorgio made shoes for the theater. He may have worked in the theater from age sixteen or seventeen until he was drafted at age twenty in 1914.

The Municipal Theater of Catanzaro / (Il Teatro Comunale Di Catanzaro)

Print of Il Teatro Comunale di Catanzaro. Date unknown. Public domain.

Most cities and towns in Italy had cultural centers that staged plays, operas, and other community-oriented events. When Giorgio was a young adult, Catanzaro had the Municipal Theater, or Il Teatro Comunale di Catanzaro. In 1830, a predecessor of the theater was built near the current Piazza Prefettura, adjacent to the Basilica of the Immaculate. *La Servi Padrone* was performed as its first opera.

A series of grand opera, prose, and other performances followed. After the unification of Italy, around 1871, the theater was rebuilt and named Teatro Comunale. The theater was a source of immense pride for the city.

During the time that Giorgio may have worked in the theater, from 1910 to 1914 (when WWI began and Giorgio was drafted), a list of performances shows a total of forty-seven operas, including *Il Travatore*, *Tosca*, *La Traviata*, *Faust*, *Geisha*, and *Don Pasquale*. Additional performances, such as plays, readings, and other community events, were also staged.

This offers insight into Giorgio's enculturation. We assume he worked in the theater's costume department, crafting shoes for the performers and being part of the in-house theater ensemble that supported visiting performance companies. In this role, the young man who grew up poor in Stilo would have been exposed to cultural experiences: people, prose, performances, and, most importantly, exquisite costumes made from rich fabrics, all highlighted by the shoes he likely crafted for the shows. If you examine photos of him from that period and throughout his life, you'll notice that he was an impeccable dresser. He almost always added a jacket, vest, tie, watch with chain, and hat. Not only was he a polished dresser, but he was a cultured bon vivant.

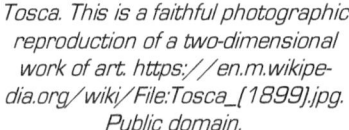

Tosca. This is a faithful photographic reproduction of a two-dimensional work of art. https://en.m.wikipedia.org/wiki/File:Tosca_[1899].jpg. Public domain.

It's fun to think of Giorgio as a "musical theater geek." He is the only person in our family with theater roots. Although not a performer, he was part of the company that staged remarkable performances before the war. And let's never underestimate the importance of shoes to a performer. We can't imagine the great sopranos and tenors at the Teatro Comunale stepping on stage without the most lavish shoes, likely designed and crafted by Giorgio. This environment is also undoubtedly where Giorgio uncovered his beautiful tenor voice.

2

Above, the image to the left is a print showing the left side of Il Teatro Comunale di Catanzaro as it appeared in 1910, approximately when Giorgio worked there. The theater featured three balconies on the side facing the road and three Roman columns in the front portico that formed the entrance. Also depicted in this print is the basilica, the building to the right and behind the theater (with the round/oval window near the top). Although it can't be seen in this picture, there was a small alley between the two structures.

The image to the right above is a contemporary photo we took in 2016. The angle differs slightly, making it hard to see the gap that was once an alley between the two buildings. To the left, in the contemporary photo, you can spot the newer building (with square windows) built where the theater once stood. The same basilica is visible on the right. Today, the structure that occupies the theater site is home to a bank kiosk and a mobile phone store at the ground level.

2

Last pictures taken inside Theatre Comunale before it was demolished in 1938. Public domain.

It was heartbreaking to see the building that replaced the site of the Teatro, which had been a cornerstone of the city's cultural life. Even in Italy, where past civilizations, works of art, and cultural heritage are celebrated and preserved, time moves on. In 1938, the theater was dismantled due to structural damage, which dealt a severe blow to the city. Later, the city built a larger, more modern theater in a different location.

From our records, we put together information about where he resided in Catanzaro. His military records indicate Vicoletto Carmine, his address before he was conscripted. To confirm his address, we discovered a letter written by his mother, Teresa DeLuca, in 1940 after he had moved to America. She listed her address on the envelope as Vico Carmine No. 6, Catanzaro. Below left is a photo of the likely place where Giorgio and his mother lived: Vico Carmine. The small sign on the side of the building reads, "Carmine."

The map of Catanzaro, below right, illustrates a route Giorgio may have taken to his job as a shoemaker for the Theatre Comunale, just a brief twelve-minute walk from his house. Alternatively, he might have gone by streetcar. This helps us to understand Giorgio's cosmopolitan life before the war.

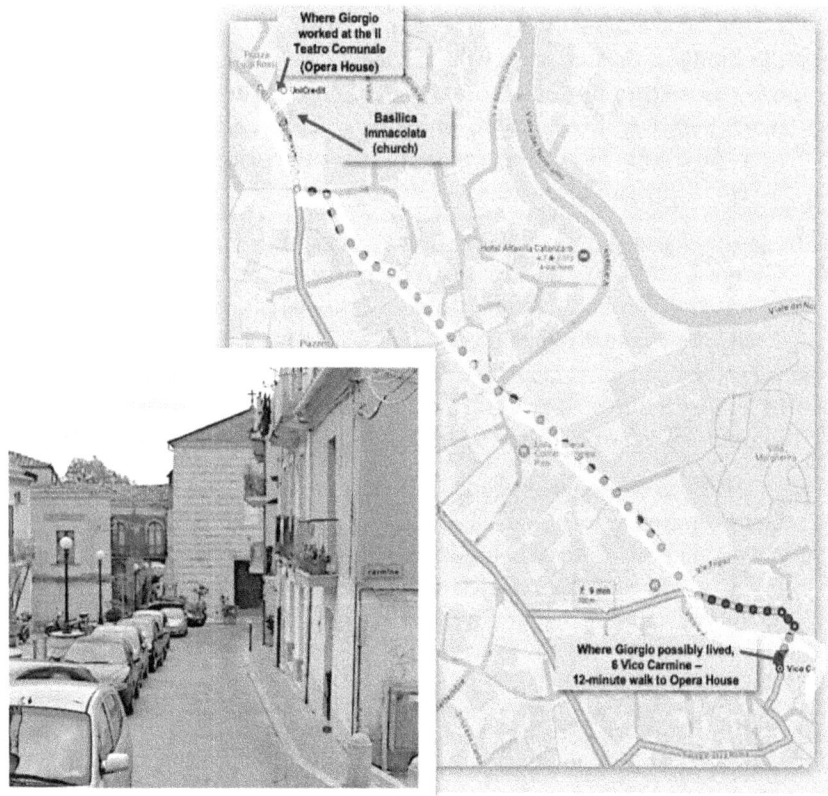

How Did Giorgio and Maria Meet?

Maria lived in Petilia Policastro, while Giorgio lived in Catanzaro, about forty miles apart—a considerable distance in those days without modern roads or public transportation. To maintain the narrative flow, our best guess is that they met a few years before he was drafted. His timeline is tight; he was drafted at twenty, meaning his apprenticeship as a shoemaker before working in the theater must have taken a few years. Anita believes that Giorgio and Maria may have met at a mutual friend's house in Catanzaro. Maria had two brothers listed on their ship's manifest as shoemakers when they emigrated to America. Perhaps they worked in Catanzaro and got to know Giorgio? The truth is, we really don't know.

We are sure they fell in love before the war. Maria once shared a heartwarming story with Anita about herself and Giorgio during their time in Italy when he worked in the theater. This story is a testament to their deep love, and it shares Giorgio's thoughtful gesture of crafting a beautiful new pair of shoes for his beloved. You can envision Giorgio pouring his heart into creating these shoes, infusing them with love for Maria.

They attended the opera, and Maria proudly wore her new shoes for the first time. However, she slipped them off and sat barefoot in the dimly lit theater during the performance. When the lights came up, she tried to put her shoes back on, but her feet had swollen so much that they no longer fit. Thinking quickly, Giorgio gallantly carried Maria to their destination, sparing her the discomfort of walking barefoot through the streets of Catanzaro.

The warm glow of Maria's shoes became a fading memory for Giorgio and Maria. The dogs of WWI began to menace Europe, and a sense of foreboding filled the air. The assassination of Austrian Archduke Franz Ferdinand on June 28, 1914, triggered a series of events that led to war in early August 1914. There was a tangible sense of unease among the young men, who were acutely aware of the looming threat of conscription.

Many young men experienced deep fear and reluctance about being drafted into a war they did not believe in. They frequently questioned the motives behind the conflict and worried for their lives in battles that felt far removed from their simple, everyday realities. As the war approached, conversations were filled with anxiety about an uncertain future. Families struggled with the possibility of losing their sons to a cause they couldn't fully understand or support. Many young men in Italy faced a profound dilemma, torn between the desire for a better life in America and the pressure to fulfill their military duties at home. The prospect of emigrating to the United States, the land of opportunity and freedom, drew numerous young Italians to dream of escaping economic hardship and political unrest. A strong national pride or a belief in the fight may have kept many from leaving. Others might have felt a moral obligation to defend their country, fearing that abandoning their duty would disgrace themselves and their families. And then there was the legal problem: if they left and did not serve, they would be listed as deserters and punished accordingly if they ever returned to Italy. Ultimately, these young men were caught in a web of conflicting loyalties and hopes, representing a poignant chapter in Italy's historical landscape during the tumultuous years leading up to the Great War.

A depiction of the assassination of Austrian Archduke Ferdinand. Public domain.

For Giorgio, his trip to America with his beloved Maria would have to wait five years. This raises questions about when they made their plan to come to America. Was it when her family began emigrating in 1907? Were they intending to go to the United States when the war disrupted their plans? Or did the horrors Giorgio would ultimately experience during his time as a soldier on the Italian front make him realize they needed to leave?

The only picture we have of Giorgio from this time, below, shows a handsome, well-dressed man who appears to be about eighteen to twenty years old, taken before the world descended into chaos.

Your Country Needs You, Mauzan, A. 1917. Italian
Credit.
*Italy, 1917. Milan, Italy: Casa Ricordi. [Photograph].
Retrieved from the Library of Congress,
https://www.loc.gov/item/2021670897/
Public domain.*

2

We don't know when Giorgio and Maria hatched their plan to emigrate to the United States, but one thing is certain: Giorgio was drafted on October 10, 1914, as the rumblings of war signaled the looming doom of what was to come.

It must have been incredibly challenging for Giorgio to endure life as a soldier during one of the most brutal and unforgiving military periods the world has ever known. Perhaps his dreams focused on Maria and crossing the Atlantic for a better life during this time.

* * *

But first, he had to survive the dogs of war.

CHAPTER 3: GIORGIO AND WORLD WAR I
1914–1919

Cry "Havoc," and let slip the dogs of war.

William Shakespeare, *Julius Caesar*

When World War I began in July 1914, Italy chose to remain neutral. However, the Italians ultimately decided to join the war against Austria-Hungary, their historical adversary, when Italy sought to acquire territory along the border of the two countries that extended from the Alps to the Adriatic Sea. Their goal was to reclaim areas with Italian-speaking populations. Shortly before the war, Italy formed alliances with the Entente powers, France and Great Britain. It negotiated the secret Pact of London, where Great Britain and France promised Italy the desired territory.

On May 3, 1915, Italy declared war on Austria-Hungary. At the beginning of the war, the Italian army comprised fewer than 300,000 soldiers, but mobilization grew to over five million by the end of November 1918. The conflict resulted in about 460,000 fatalities and 955,000 wounded. Giorgio was among the injured, but we are getting ahead of our story.

The Italian army was established in 1861 and was based on conscription, which mandated military service for all males aged eighteen to forty-five; the older conscripts were assigned to noncombat jobs. Being called up represented, among other things, the nationalization of the divided country now under the Italian king. Thus, conscription signified the new national state's power to intervene in the lives of its citizens. However, many Italians, particularly those in the southern regions, did not welcome conscription, feeling marginalized by the North. Officer ranks were designated for the social elite, mostly excluding Southern Italians. It's fair to say that the army was not a popular institution. In 1910, this unpopularity led to a reduction of national service to only two years. Draftees often failed to report, even during WWI. The classes—the military code for categories of soldiers grouped by birth year—called up in September 1915 and April 1916 had a 12 percent evasion rate.

In 1915, the Italian army consisted of 96 infantry regiments, which grew to 236 during the war. These regiments were recruited by region and then strategically assigned to areas outside their original locations to move soldiers around the country. Each regiment was reassigned to a new location every three to five years. The army was seen as a vital tool for "Italianization."

Even amidst the turmoil of conscription and Italianization, many were proud to serve their country. Surviving letters offer insight into soldiers' thoughts about the war. One such soldier was twenty-four-year-old Amadeo Rossi, a shoemaker from the Cesena region:

> *Every day today we suffer for the fatherland. And it is our duty, as our old people did in times past. And today our duty awaits us towards our beautiful Italy, and we shall not let them call us cowards but on the contrary heroes for all time of history.*

3

The conscription records, also known as Liste di Leva, indicate the board's final decisions regarding each individual's fitness for military service. Ineligibility was mainly determined by poor health, disability, and criminal records. This was the first war in Italy where comprehensive written records were kept on soldiers. Most of the records are handwritten and not even typed. A vital record known as Foglio Matricolare (military curriculum of a draftee) tracked each soldier's military career, including changes in status, promotions, and final discharge. Giorgio's Foglio Matricolare is shown on the next page.

Giorgio's Foglio Matricolare & Caratteristico 1914–1918.
(Military Curriculum & Characteristics)

Some Italians already in the United States returned to Italy to serve. At the same time, many more stayed in the United States and were labeled deserters, a fact often noted on their retained military records. This might explain why some of our male ancestors took a long time to return to Italy after the war; after all, desertion was punishable by imprisonment or even death. On the other hand, many Italian immigrants, including some of our male ancestors, pledged their loyalty to America and fought as part of the American military.

We don't know Giorgio's political views or when he and Maria formulated their plan to come to the United States; it's possible that they finalized their plans when the war broke out and Giorgio was called to serve. Given that many of Maria's family members had already emigrated, it stands to reason that their ideas about where and how to go stemmed from her siblings' experiences on their journey to the United States. It is admirable that Giorgio stayed and fought for Italy from 1914 to 1919, particularly if one assumes that he disagreed with Italy's direction.

On September 6, 1914, the military conducted a mandatory criminal background check on Giorgio. The results revealed no criminal records. On September 10, 1914, Giorgio was called up. He was living in Catanzaro, and his occupation was listed as a shoemaker. On October 10, 1914, at age twenty, Giorgio reported for duty. His military registration number was 44319 from Reggio Calabria, the region of his birth. He belonged to the class of 1894. As was customary, many of his military records identified Giorgio by his name, military registration number, class (birth year), and his father's first name, Dominico. The records occasionally listed his mother, Teresa DeLuca.

A standard induction form listed Giorgio as unmarried and his physical characteristics: *unmarried*, height *5 feet 3 inches*, chest *36 inches*, hair color *black*, hair type *wavy*, nose *big*, chin *large*, eyes *black*, complexion *brown*, forehead *broad*, mouth *small*, face *oval*, and abilities *good*.

Giorgio was in training from October 10, 1914 (when he reported for duty) until July 6, 1915, although his military records do not specify the location. By 1915, the additional characteristics noted in his military records indicated that he was very robust, his conduct was good in-service and excellent out-of-service, he took sufficient care of the equipment he was assigned, and his military training was sufficient.

His induction form also states that he was unable to read or write. Subsequent military records from 1915 indicate that he "can't read well" and that his education was "poor." This, of course, referred to reading and writing in his native language, Italian. By the time he boarded the ship to the United States in 1920, he was listed as able to read and write. This might suggest that he learned these skills in the military. It could also mean he was somewhat loose with the facts when asked about his reading and writing abilities on the ship. Anita recalls that his reading and writing abilities in English and Italian in the 1940s in America were poor. Maria wrote all the letters to their Italian relatives.

Cavalleggeri (Cavalrymen) di Treviso 28th

The Cavalleggeri di Treviso (28th) Regiment was formed in Florence on October 1, 1909. The regiment had its unique coat of arms, as

shown to the left. It consisted of three sections, with the Tarvisium (for Treviso) separating three castles in the top right segment from a walled gate in the lower right segment. A crown adorns the entire coat of arms. The banner at the bottom, translated from Latin, reads "Brave in the Struggle." The gorget patches shown to the right of the coat of arms were worn on a uniform collar to signify the unit.

By July 6, 1915, at age twenty-one, Giorgio arrived in his first combat zone, again with no indication of his location in his records. A new machine gun section, composed of men from the 28th, was attached to the 60th Division. However, his records show a blemish, the first of two. On July 6, 1915, he was punished for a violation related to his post. It appears that he fell asleep on duty, although the record is difficult to read. Regardless, it was a serious offense for which he received five days in jail.

The next entry in his records shows that he left the combat zone on November 11, 1915, and was reassigned to another combat zone. Things were not looking up. On May 23, 1916, he was deployed in the sector east of Monfalcone, Italy.

The Battle of Monfalcone

The year 1916 was significant for Giorgio. His regiment was stationed on the Austro-Hungarian front along the northern Alpine border in the Trentino region, in the mountainous area of the Isonzo River (now in Slovenia), and their stationing extended down toward the Adriatic. This was known as the Isonzo or Italian Front. Italian forces suffered tremendous casualties from 1915 to 1917, particularly during poorly managed and botched attempts to break the enemy on the Isonzo Front.

The Italian military at the Isonzo Front was notorious for military blunders and mismanagement. On May 24, 1916, an Italian battery sustained heavy casualties: a hundred soldiers were killed by friendly fire. The battery commanders did not learn to coordinate their fire with infantry advances until the following summer. The losses around Monfalcone were nearly three hundred.

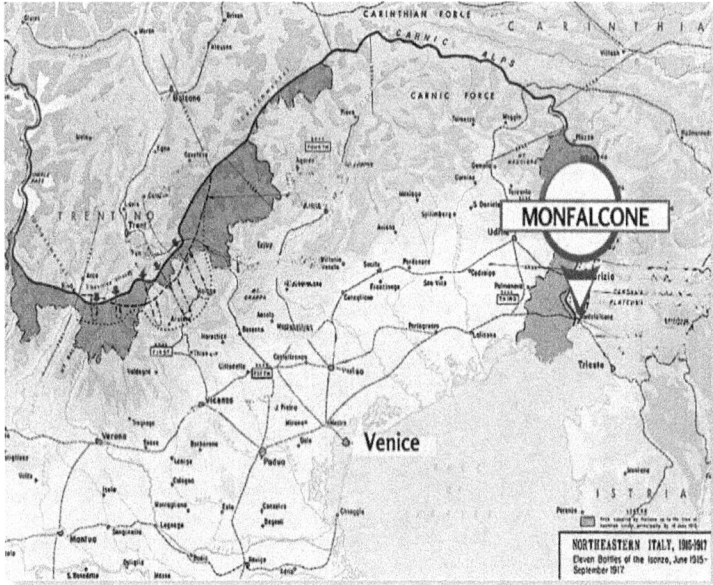

The Italian WWI front lines map shows Monfalcone, Italy. Public domain.

On June 9, 1916, the Italians engaged in combat for the first time with the Austrians on the lower Isonzo River at Sagrado, a small town southwest of Gorizia. Before dawn, a battalion from the Pisa Brigade crossed a pontoon bridge set up across the river, aided by a sandy islet in midstream that made the crossing easier. (The islet is still visible today.) The Italian artillery pounded the enemy's forward positions across the river. The pontoon bridge was destroyed, leaving the battalion stranded without supplies or support. The Italians fell back to the river and resorted to using bayonets when their ammunition ran out. As the Austrians closed in, they deployed new weapons that the Italians had never encountered—hand grenades.

The Italians waded back to the small island, where the water was only three feet deep, digging into the sand as best they could. At nightfall, the handful of survivors struggled back to the western shore, leaving behind about five hundred dead. It was an astonishing blunder among a series of staggering blunders by the Italian military officers on the Isonzo Front. It must have been genuinely demoralizing to exert so much effort only to be at the mercy of so many incompetent, life-threatening military decisions.

Giorgio's regiment fought in the trenches during the Battle of Monfalcone. As noted in 1916, he was wounded by enemy fire on June 16. No further details are available about his injuries or recovery. He received a citation stating:

> *After being present at the Battle of Monfalcone, which included a cavalry engagement, he was awarded the bronze medal for military valor.*

Giorgio Simonetti

Europe War (WWI) 1915-1918
Cavalleggeri (Cavalrymen) di Treviso (28th)

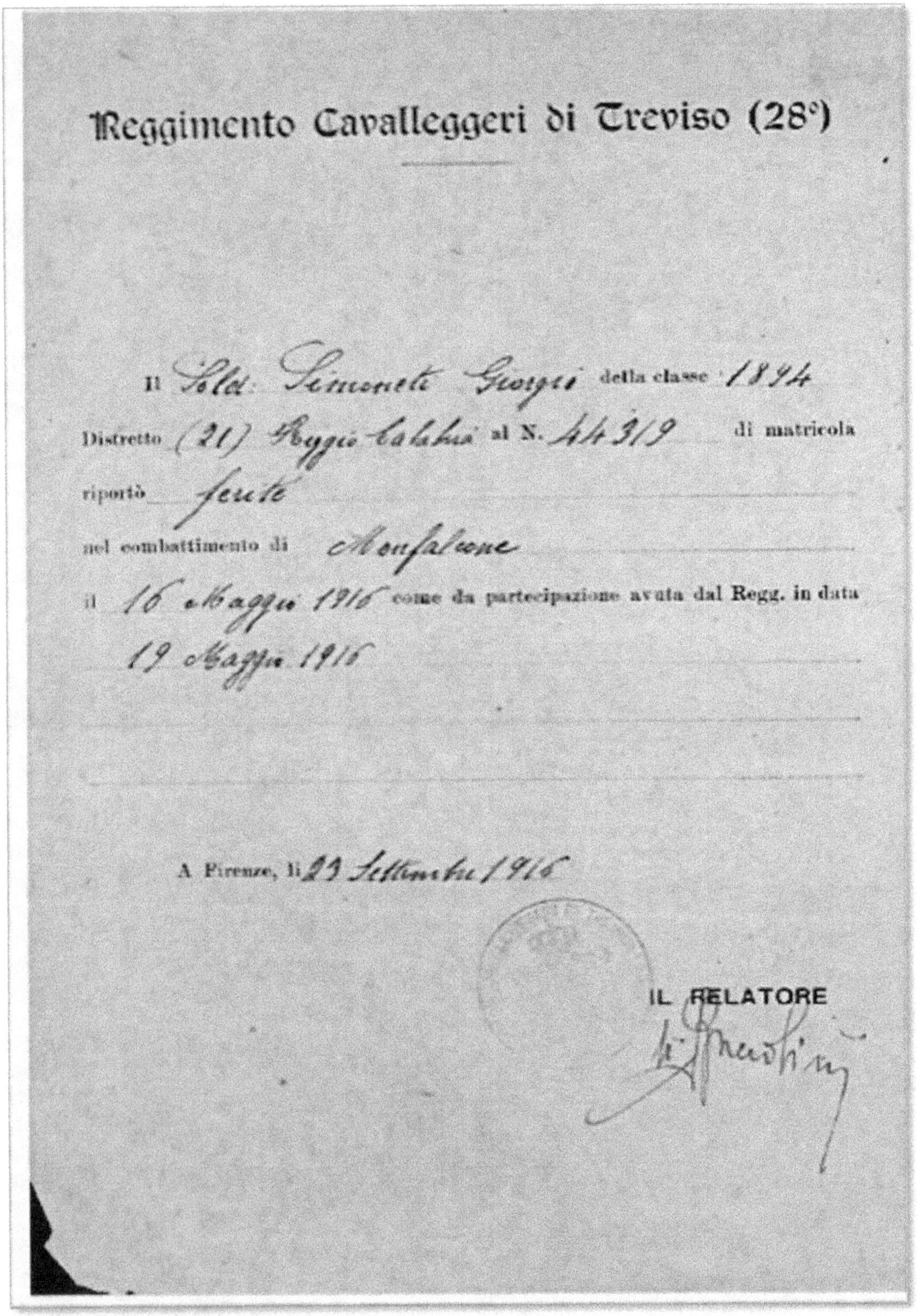

Reggimento Cavalleggeri di Treviso (28°)

Il *Sold: Simonetti Giorgio* della classe *1894*

Distretto *(21) Reggio Calabria* al N. *44319* di matricola

riportò *ferite*

nel combattimento di *Monfalcone*

il *16 Maggio 1916* come da partecipazione avuta dal Regg. in data

19 Maggio 1916

A Firenze, li *23 Settembre 1916*

IL RELATORE

Military report that shows Giorgio was wounded at the Battle of Monfalcone. Family archives.

The trenches dug into the bare rock of the Carnic mountain range, part of the southern Alps, and on the slopes of Monfalcone during the battles of 1915–1917 are well preserved today. They can be found on the high plateaus behind Monfalcone in what is now a WWI re-membrance park (Parco Tematico della Grande Guerra).

Giorgio's regiment departed from the Isonzo region on September 19, 1916. From April 25, 1917, Giorgio's war records show he was moved from one combat zone to another, but the records do not say where.

Giorgio was trained as a machine gunner and assigned to the Tre-viso Cavalry Regiment (28th), most likely starting in 1917, when the regimental depot in Florence formed the 734th Dismounted Machine Gunners Company to reinforce infantry units on the front.

Giorgio's military medal in family archives. Photo by Justin Maynard.

One medal he received, shown above, depicts his machine gun. He was likely assigned a Fiat-Revelli model 1914, Italy's main machine gun of the war. Its magazines held fifty rounds (6.5 mm). The weapon weighed eighty-five pounds with the tripod. In theory its rate of fire was five hundred rounds per minute, but in fact it fired about four hundred rounds per minute. Like many machine guns of that period, it was water-cooled and somewhat cumbersome. Moving and setting up the machine gun in the frigid mountain regions was torturous. Giorgio was likely on the front lines in every conflict he participated in, making his time at war perilous. As a machine gunner, he was likely responsible for the deaths of many enemy soldiers, not necessarily through hand-to-hand combat, but close enough to suffer post-traumatic stress from the casualties his gun no doubt caused.

During the retreat from Caporetto, the regiment was tasked with gathering stragglers in the Treviso area and subsequently crossing the Piave River at Vidor under the command of the 3rd Army.

Then something unbecoming happened.

On September 9, 1918, Giorgio and a companion were punished for "indecent acts contrary to regulation." His war records provide only a one-sentence entry. We do not know what the indecent act was or where it occurred. All we know is that he received five days in military prison, suitable for a serious offense.

On October 29, 1917, after crossing the Piave River, the entire 28th Treviso Cavalry Regiment was dispatched to pursue the retreating enemy; the battle of Vittorio Veneto was underway. One hundred thirty-eight enemy officers from Treviso were taken prisoner, and over 3,300 troops, 24 cannons, 302 horses, 101 wagons, 2,700 rifles, and 42 machine guns were captured.

Amidst all this wartime chaos, the Spanish flu epidemic struck in early 1918, infecting five hundred soldiers in the 28th, thirty of whom died. However, this misery was about to come to an end. The armistice was signed on November 11, 1918. At that time, Giorgio's regiment was fighting in Carpenedo. After Carpenedo, his regiment returned to headquarters in Florence. We do not have records of his military assignments from November 11, 1918, to the following year. He was discharged on September 12, 1919, and his final pay was issued on September 19, 1919. After five long years, he could finally go home.

* * *

Giorgio and Maria were now sojourners, ready to head west to a new life.

Giorgio Simonetti discharge papers, September 12, 1919.
Family archives.

3

Giorgio in his Cavalleggeri di Treviso (28th) military uniform. Note the machine gunner patch on his sleeve. Family archives.

It was an eerie feeling to be the first to read Giorgio's military records in over 110 years. It occurred to me that even Giorgio did not know what they contained. Now his granddaughter, whom he never met, was reading about the trials and tribulations of his military service—his permanent record, so to speak—without redactions or edits.

Hello, Giorgio! Nice to meet you. I learned that you could not read or write during your service. You took good (not great) care of the equipment assigned to you. When given a choice to mark a regular-sized nose or a big nose, the Italian enlisted man looking you over to complete the "physical characteristics" portion of your records chose "big nose." Your forehead was broad, your mouth was small, your face shape was oval, and your eyebrows were thick. (We are indeed related.) Your complexion was brown. You were very robust, your conduct was good (until it wasn't), your military training was "sufficient" (ouch), and your aptitude for advancement was left blank. (ouch, ouch). You were imprisoned twice: once for leaving your post without permission or falling asleep at your post, depending on which translation is correct. Your second offense is shrouded in mystery: indecent acts contrary to regulation. Well, that could mean anything! Giorgio, good to know that you were not perfect, just a regular guy trying to fulfill your duty to a country you would soon leave behind.

There is uncertainty about whether we can truly understand ourselves. Why do we what we do? What drives us? What are the reasons behind our actions? What arrogance leads us to believe we can travel back in time and attempt to understand another person? Even professional genealogists, with greater resources and knowledge than us amateurs, can only piece together a thin veil of someone's life. This veil is filled with gaps, assumptions, leaps of faith, and unanswerable questions. We work with what we have, and somehow it forms a picture. It's like using a microscope to observe the skies: you only see a tiny sample, with the vast majority remaining unknowable. Yet, it's all we have. We do our best. It comforts us to have even a slight understanding of our ancestors and their lives. Even a fragment of understanding has the power to change who we are.

CHAPTER 4: MOON IN THE MIDDLE
OF THE SEA
1920–1921

There's the moon in the middle of the sea; there's a moon in the middle of the sea:
Mother, I must get married. My daughter, who do I get for you?
Mother, I leave it up to you.

Southern Italian folk song: "C'e La Luna Mezz'o Mare,"
a song Maria used to sing in Italian to the authors as children.

The decision to leave Italy and immigrate to America involved a risky journey for Giorgio and Maria. Letters from family members already in the United States likely portrayed Rivesville, West Virginia, as the Emerald City—filled with jobs, food, and housing. Safe neighborhoods, freedom, and independence might have been highlighted. No earthquakes, volcanoes, or horrific natural disasters. Like their homeland, the area offered beautiful mountains, trees, and meadows. However, the road ahead would be challenging. Giorgio and Maria's journey involved thousands of miles across land and sea, and their passage was not easy. Understanding their journey emphasizes their strength and courage. Their sacrifices to start anew and build a family in America are not lost on the authors.

By Rail from Catanzaro to Naples

Preparation was necessary before their journey. Maria's sixty-three-year-old mother, Rosa, would also be traveling with them, and they would be saying goodbye to family members without knowing if they would ever see each other again. They needed photos for keepsakes and family memorabilia. They booked their travel and ensured they had all the proper documentation, tickets, and fees. They also had to consider what belongings to take that would fit in one steamer trunk and any small cloth bags they could carry. Giorgio decided to tuck his favorite cobbler's hammer into his bag. He named her Aria (an operatic solo that expresses a character's feelings), perhaps because she was an essential part of his craft. She was the perfect hammer, balanced and heavy enough to do the job well. Aria's shape and weight fit perfectly in his hand. They also packed small toiletries for personal care. They needed food and water in case they couldn't find nourishment along the way. And they had to ensure their clothing had multiple pockets to conceal money and valuables from thieves and con artists. All this preparation for a challenging and monumental thirty-day journey.

Travelers at the train station in Catanzaro, Italy, 1920.
Public domain.

4

Once Giorgio, Maria, and Rosa had their business in order and their bags packed, they began the first leg of their journey. They likely traveled from a train station in Catanzaro and headed northwest toward Naples, Italy. The train ride up to the Italian Mediterranean coast spanned about three hundred miles. They journeyed by train through the coastal towns of Paola, Scalera, Maratea, and Battaglia. Having traveled long distances by train during his military service, Giorgio was accustomed to the lengthy ride and the barren landscapes. However, this might have been Maria and Rosa's first trip out of Catanzaro. Giorgio's travel experience likely helped Maria and Rosa appreciate the ride and the scenery. The train continued traveling north through Salerno and Pompei, and then it finally reached the Port of Naples. The trip may have taken two to three days, depending on the number of stops or delays. We, the authors, note that nearly one hundred years later, in 2016, we followed the same train tracks from Catanzaro to Naples, albeit on a modern train in business class, through contemporary passages with modern amenities.

Once at the Port of Naples, Giorgio, Maria, and Rosa disembarked from the train. At the port, their names were recorded on the manifest (the ship's log of passengers), so their tickets must have been purchased in advance. They were preparing for the next leg, which would be the longest journey of their lives.

Sailing from the Port of Naples

At the Port of Naples, Giorgio, Maria, and Rosa were likely part of a crowd of thousands. People carried bags, coats, hats, and gloves. Tired children cried, fussy from their busy travel schedules. Amidst the crowds, Giorgio, Maria, and Rosa boarded the steamship S.S. Braga on December 16, 1920. The ship's crew checked the names on the manifest. According to the ship's records, there were fifty-five pages listing about thirty passengers per page. A few passengers were classified as special class, likely first class. Some special class passengers who traveled in luxury included Carlo Ghelardi, the Italian Royal Commissioner (diplomat), and the d'Avella family from Long Island, New York. There was an estimated count of 1,204 aliens (the term for non-US immigrants), who were mainly third-class passengers. The ship employed a crew of 120 from many different nations. The manifests contained extensive information for each passenger.

Port of Naples 1915. Public domain.

S.S. Braga—The ship that Giorgio, Maria, and Rosa sailed on to the United States in 1920–1921. Public domain.

COL. NO.	U.S. DEPARTMENT OF LABOR LIST 8	GIORGIO SIMONETTI	ROSA BENINCASA	MARIA RASPA
1	No. of List - Line Number	4	5	6
2	Head Tax Status	-	-	-
3	Family Name	Simonetti	Benincasa	Raspa
	Given Name	Giorgio	Rosa	Maria
		(Handwritten "son in law")	(Handwritten "R")	Handwritten "daughter"
4	Age	26	63	22
5	Sex	M	F	F
6	Marital Status	S (single)	W (widow)	S (single)
7	Occupation	Shoemaker	Peasant	Domestic
8	Read	Yes	No	Yes
	What Language	Italian	Rejoins her son	Italian
	Write	Yes	Not Listed	Yes
9	Nationality	Italy	Italy	Italy
10	Race	So. Italian	So. Italian	So. Italian
11	Last Permanent Address County City or Town	Italy Catanzaro	Italy Catanzaro	Italy Catanzaro
12	Name/Address of Nearest Relative	His mother Teresa DeLuca, Catanzaro	She leaves none	She leaves none
13	Final Destination State, City	W. Va. Rivesville	N.Y. Riversville	N.Y. Riversville
14	No. on List – Line Number	4	5	6
15	Whether having a ticket to such final destination.	No	No	No
16	By whom was paid? (Whether alien paid his own passage, whether paid by relative, whether paid by any other person, or by any corporation, society, municipality or government)	Himself	Herself	Herself
17	Whether in Possession of $50, and if less, how much?	$50	$60	$20
18	Whether ever before in the U.S.? If so, when and where?	No	No	NO
19	If joining a relative or friend; what relative or friend; name and complete address.	His brother-in-law Francesco Raspa, Box 511 Rivesville, W.Va.	Her son Francesco Raspa, Box 511 Riversville, N.Y.	Her brother Francesco Raspa, Box 511 Riversville, N.Y.
20	Purpose of coming to U.S. A - Whether alien intends to return to county whence. B - Length of time alien intends to remain in the U.S. C - Whether alien intends to become a citizen of the U.S.	A – No B – Always C - Yes	A – No B – Always C - Yes	A – No B – Always C - Yes
21	Ever in prison or altercation or indentation for care or treatment of the insane or supported by charity. If so, which?	No	No	No
22	Whether a polygamist.	No	No	No
23	Whether an anarchist.	No	No	No
24	Whether a person who believes in or advocates the overthrow by force or violence of the Government of the U.S. or all forms of law, etc.	No	No	No
25	Whether coming by any reason of any offer, activism, promise or agreement express or complied to labor in the U.S.	No	No	No
26	Whether alien had been previously deported within one year.	No	No	No
27	Condition of health, mental and physical.	Good "med. Cert. senility might have been detected at foreign post"	Good	Good
28	Deformed or crippled. Nature, length of time and cause.	No	No	No
29	Height, Feet, Inches	5'4"	5'5"	5'5"
30	Complexation	Fair	Fair	Fair
31	Color of Hair	Black	Gray	Brown
	Color of Eyes	Chestnut	Chestnut	Chestnut
32	Marks of identification.	None	None	None
33	Place of Birth, Country	Italy,	Italy,	Italy,
	City or Town	Cantanzaro	Cantanzaro	Petilia Policastro

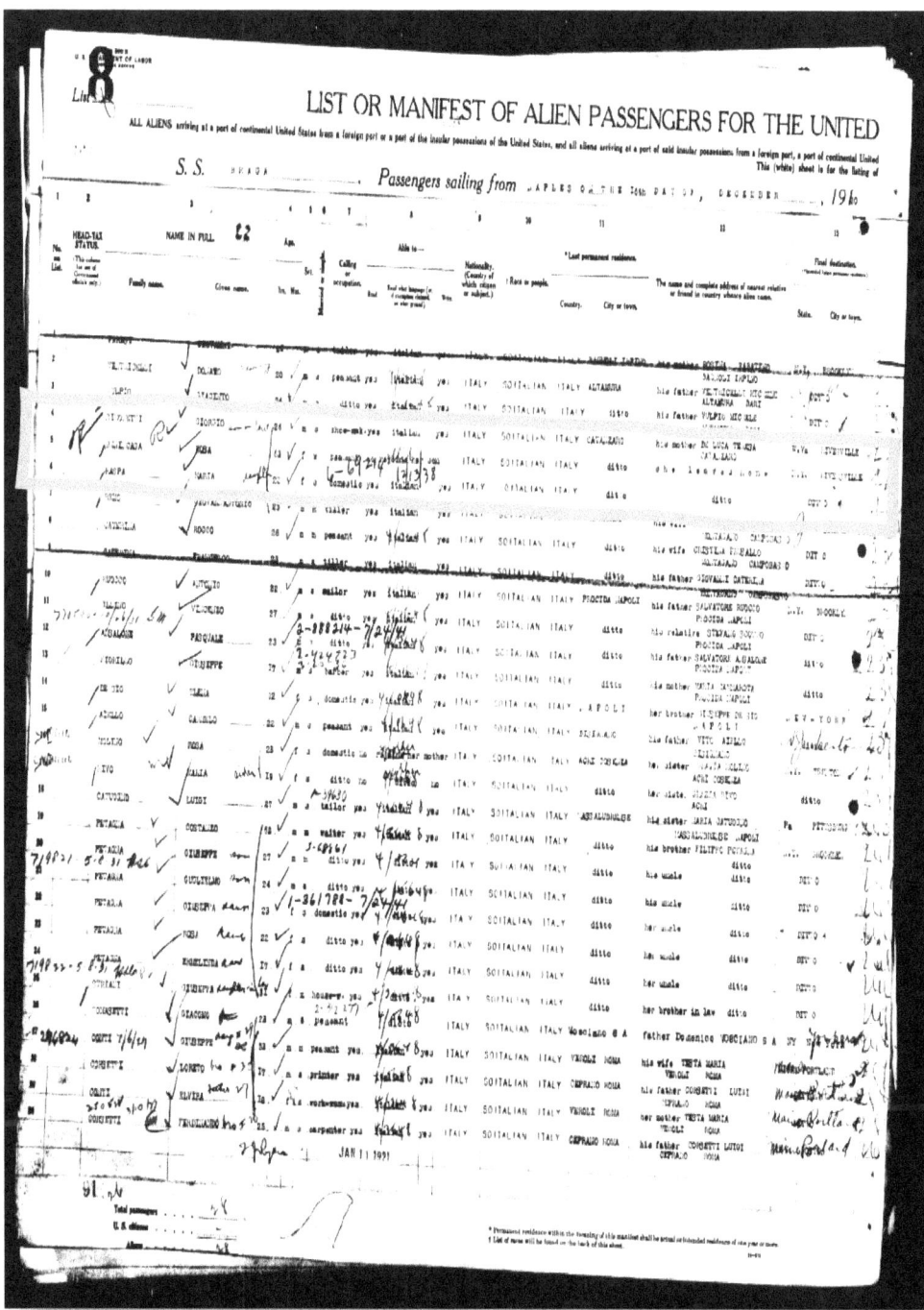

Were Giorgio and Maria married when they boarded the ship? The manifest indicates Giorgio and Maria as single or "s." However, a handwritten note next to Giorgio's name states "son-in-law," indicating his relationship with Rosa and that he was married. Another family story suggests that Maria's older brother, Frank Raspa, arranged a marriage for her when she arrived in America. Maria and Giorgio likely had a civil ceremony in Italy to avoid complications of the arranged marriage in America. We have not found a marriage license in Italy, but because of these family tales, Anita believes that Giorgio and Maria married before going to America.

Once aboard the ship, they likely made their way to the "classification" area. As peasants, their classification was probably third-class or "steerage." On a steamship, steerage represented the cheapest and lowest class of travel. Passengers in steerage were directed to the ship's lower decks that sat below the waterline. Unlike first or second-class passengers, steerage offered no magnificent ocean views. The steerage halls were filled with rows of metal bunks stacked two high. The bunk areas were old, worn, unsanitary, and claustrophobic. It's possible that men and women were kept in separate quarters.

Privacy was virtually nonexistent. Amenities were few and far between. Rooms in steerage were minimal. Areas for sitting and socializing were likely open spaces crowded with hundreds of people. Bath facilities were shared, and bathrooms probably afforded little privacy for men and women aboard the ship. These public bathrooms and toilets were undoubtedly filthy, contributing to the sickness and, in some cases, deaths of passengers. Travelers likely experienced motion sickness and struggled to quickly reach bathroom facilities rapidly. Ventilation was inadequate, increasing the likelihood of airborne viruses and illnesses spreading among passengers. The threat of diseases such as cholera, dysentery, yellow fever, smallpox, or typhus was rampant. Living below the ship's deck, steerage passengers were probably close to the loud, roaring steam engines. The incessant humming and vibration from the engines and the ship's movement through the water were likely unbearable for those in steerage. Some steerage passengers could go onto the deck for fresh air depending on the weather. However, for Giorgio and Maria, the open air of the Atlantic Sea was freezing as they traveled in late December and early January.

The bedding consisted of straw mattresses and a canvas sheet. The pillow was a life preserver. The ship likely provided the blankets and metal utensils, which included a fork and spoon in a tin lunch pail. The immigrants relied on the rations they brought or the ship's unappetizing meals. Eating facilities resembled cafeteria tables or benches. Each family took turns eating in the area. After one family finished, the next would take over the table or bench. Or perhaps they had to eat on the floor. Giorgio, Maria, and Rosa spent twenty days on the S.S. Braga, nearly three weeks. Considering today's creature comforts, we can only imagine the ordeal of traveling under such conditions.

Passengers on a ship's deck. https://picryl.com/media/immi-grants-on-an-atlantic-liner. Public domain.

4

The S.S. Braga's journey from Naples, Italy, to New York City followed a long and treacherous route. After departing from the Port of Naples, the ship was directed west through the Tyrrhenian Sea, part of the Mediterranean Sea. It traveled past the southern and northern tips of several countries and territories, including southern Sardinia, northern Algeria, northern Morocco, and the southern tip of Spain. Upon reaching southern Spain and northern Morocco, they sailed through the famous Strait of Gibraltar, the key waterway connecting the Mediterranean Sea to the Atlantic Ocean. This strait separates two continents, Europe and Africa, by nine miles. At this point, the S.S. Braga had covered 1,310 miles.

The ship was then steered into the wide-open northern Atlantic Ocean, passing near the islands of Portugal and into the colder marine waters. They were sailing in late December, and the ship's areas were probably freezing, requiring a heavy coat, gloves, and hat for comfort. It's uncertain how their living quarters were heated, knowing that third class or steerage provided fewer amenities for comfort. The S.S. Braga sailed near where the famous Titanic had sunk into the frigid

Atlantic waters just a few years earlier in April 1912. It's unclear whether the ship had to navigate around icebergs or if anyone on the S.S. Braga remembered the famous maritime tragedy as they passed through the icy waters of the North Atlantic.

Arriving at the Golden Door

View of the Statue of Liberty from an immigrant's ship, early 1900s.
https://picryl.com/media/immigrants-approaching-statue-of-liberty.
Public domain.

After sailing 2,425 nautical miles through the chilly northern Atlantic waters, Giorgio, Maria, and Rosa finally glimpsed the United States and the Statue of Liberty. They had endured the voyage from Italy to America.

Giorgio, Maria, and Rosa probably had a combination of emotions. Tired from the long travel days, eager to get off the ship, and afraid of entering a new country with different languages and customs, they must have been uncertain if they would successfully pass through one of the final legs of their journey.

The large S.S. Braga likely docked near the lower Hudson River, as larger vessels could not navigate the upper, narrower bay between New Jersey and lower Manhattan. With their bags and belongings in hand, Giorgio, Maria, and Rosa exited the steamship and probably boarded a ferry to take them to the famous Ellis Island. At sixty-three, Rosa must have been exhausted. Maria and Giorgio likely showed great care in assisting Rosa through this demanding ordeal.

Herded, Prodded, and Scrutinized at Ellis Island

Ellis Island, New York. https://picryl.com/media/colliers-1921-new-york-city-immigration-station-on-ellis-island-cdf887. Public domain.

Once the ferry docked, the passengers proceeded to the infamous Ellis Island. As they walked into the echoing dark halls, anxious about the next step, they were greeted by immigration officers shouting orders. Many Italians did not understand what the officials said, so they followed the crowd. Giorgio, Maria, and Rosa did exactly that, taking their only belongings with them. They then climbed the grand staircase to the infamous "Great Hall." The registry room featured a large dome-shaped ceiling with windows lining the walls. A giant American flag hung at the front of the hall. Benches were placed on either side of the room. The uniformed health officers watched everyone closely for any signs of heart issues, breathing difficulties, or other disabilities.

This was the first fitness test for immigrants. They would then be questioned by the US Immigration Bureau officers, who asked questions such as why they were coming to the United States, how they intended to support themselves, and their destination. They might also inquire about political beliefs and other relevant information.

Ellis Island, the Great Hall. https://picryl.com/media/immigrants-seated-on-long-benches-main-hall-us-immigration-station-8d958c. Public domain.

Some of these questions are listed on Maria and Giorgio's ship manifest, as previously noted. The time required for processing would depend on how many ships docked that day and the number of people in line.

The primary concern was passing the medical inspections. Chalk marks on the immigrants' clothing indicated a medical condition. (E) for eye problems, (H) for heart issues, and (L) for lameness were among the conditions marked. Other listed conditions included (C) conjunctivitis, (Pg) pregnancy, (Ct) trachoma, (S) senility, and (X) mental disorder. United States law mandated that physicians conduct intelligence exams to identify "idiots, imbeciles, morons, or other mentally deficient persons." Immigrants labeled with minor illnesses were detained for a few days, while those with more severe medical conditions were separated and likely deported.

The doctors in the next group were the dreaded eye specialists. These physicians examined patients for any eye diseases, such as trachoma. Trachoma was a severe disease, with three out of four victims left blind. Of all the exams the immigrants had to endure, the eye exam was the worst. Some physicians used a buttonhook to turn the person's eyelid outward; others used their index finger.

The dreaded eye men examining immigrants at Ellis Island.
https://picryl.com/media/ellis-island-ny-line-inspection-of-arriving-
aliens-657823. Public domain.

After a few hours of processing and medical exams, most of the immigrants at Ellis Island were free to go. There is a faintly remembered family story in which Giorgio was pulled aside for additional inspection, so Maria and Rosa had to wait for him to be cleared. It might be related to the manifest leaving Naples, Italy, that noted about Giorgio: "medical certified senility might have been detected at foreign post." Whatever the reason, Maria and Rosa must have been terrified. Eventually, Giorgio, Maria, and Rosa continued to the next leg of their journey, heading toward West Virginia.

By Rail to West Virginia

At this point, Giorgio, Maria, and Rosa had been traveling for a grueling five weeks straight. They spent two or three days on a train from Catanzaro to Naples and then took a steamship from Naples to New York City in December and January, which must have been both scary and exhausting. Giorgio and Maria were in their twenties, so they might have been more tolerant of the conditions. However, Rosa, Maria's mother, was sixty-three years old. They likely took a ferry from Ellis Island into New York City. It's unclear where they may have stayed to rest after their long journey.

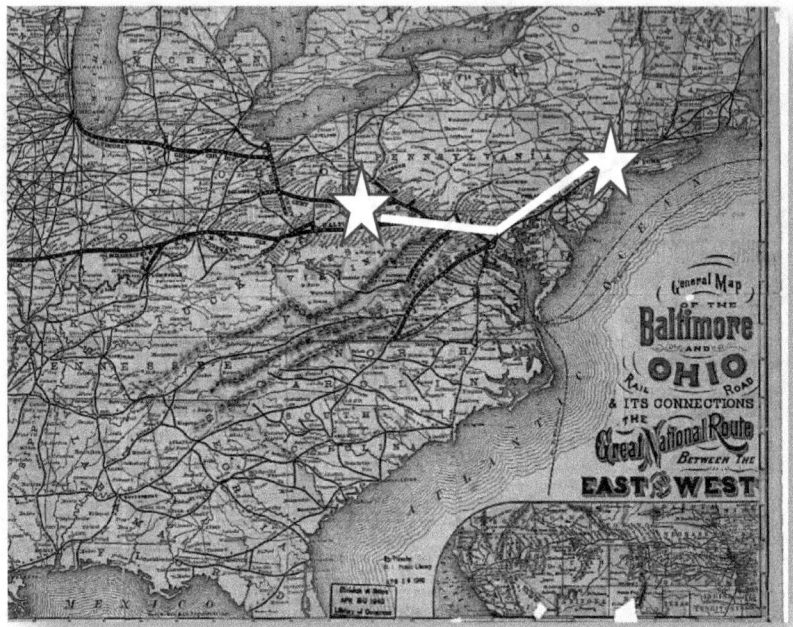

Baltimore and Ohio Train route from New York to West Virginia.
circa 1920. Public domain.

4

Several passengers on the S.S. Braga's manifest were also going to West Virginia, so possibly they traveled from New York with Giorgio, Maria, and Rosa. We don't know how they traveled from New York to West Virginia. They probably took a train from the Pennsylvania (Penn) Train Station in New York City to Fairmont, West Virginia.

Their final eight-hundred-mile train trip likely traveled through Philadelphia, Pennsylvania, then to Baltimore and Cumberland, Maryland, before continuing to Keyser, Oakland, Kingwood, Grafton, and finally Fairmont, West Virginia. Traveling by train in January 1921 may have caused them to face several weather delays through the Appalachian Mountain regions and cities.

While traveling on their final leg, Giorgio and Maria might have discussed how grateful they were that their arduous journey was nearly over. They must have felt physically and emotionally drained. During their long trip, there was ample time to reflect on the sadness of leaving behind family, friends, and their homeland.

But with that sorrow came joy. Giorgio and Maria soon started a new life together in America, with a family already settled in their new hometown. The fatigue, sadness, and joy must have contributed to an intense emotional roller-coaster.

But on the journey, the emotional rollercoaster was taking them up and down the hills and valleys of Pennsylvania on their way to a new home in the Appalachian Mountains. They must have had a million questions: *Did we make the right choice? What will our new home be like? Will we find jobs to support ourselves and our future family? Now that we've bet everything, will our lives improve? Does the Italy we left behind forgive us? Will America welcome us?*

How long until we see the families we left behind?

When Giorgio, Maria, and Rosa stepped off the train in Fairmont, West Virginia, the closest station to their destination of Rivesville, they must have breathed a sigh of relief and known that they were home. No doubt Maria's brother, Frank, greeted them at the station.

Fairmont, West Virginia, train station circa 1920. Public domain.

Finally, after their long and arduous journey, Giorgio, Maria, and Rosa had arrived. It's hard to imagine how glad they must have been to rest and finally get to know their new home. They could start fresh and pursue their dreams of a better life in America. However, they soon realized that the streets were not *actually* paved with gold. Instead, they might have noticed the coal cinders, black and sparkly, used in West Virginia to treat icy winter roads.

* * *

While not the same as finding gold, the roads must have sparkled with the promise of dreams of a better life in a new land.

My grandfather died before I was born. Growing up, I really did not know my grandmother. She spoke very little English, and I spoke zero Italian, so communicating was difficult. My grandmother raised five children and several grandchildren in a small four-room house. She had friends and family throughout her neighborhood. When I visited, I knew that Rivesville, West Virgina, was a special place, yet I didn't understand just how special my grandmother was.

My grandmother was twenty-three, my grandfather was twenty-six, and my great-grandmother was sixty-three when they traveled the four-thousand-mile trip from Catanzaro, Italy, to Rivesville, West Virginia, across roads, rails, and ocean. They had to say goodbye to their family and friends, fearing they would never see them again. They could only carry a few belongings. They left so many memories behind. They sailed on the frigid waters of the northern Atlantic Ocean for twenty days in the dead of winter.

They lived on a steamer with a thousand other passengers, uncomfortable beds, minimal bathing, tasteless food, and people all around just trying to survive the trip. Some did not. It's unimaginable. They landed in the United States, unable to speak the language, and somehow made it through the infamous travails of Ellis Island. They found food and a place to rest in New York City, navigated to the train station, and sat on a train for almost a week to reach West Virginia. How did they do that? How did they endure such an arduous trip?

Growing up, I never heard a word about their trip. My grandmother may not have wanted to talk about such an ordeal. But I wish I would have asked. To listen to her stories, memories, fears, and regrets. To look at her pictures as she talked about family and Italy. To ask about the old radio in her living room and how my grandfather played his Mario Lanza opera records. Or the cross on her bedroom wall. The letters she wrote to and received from family members in Italy. How she fell in love with my grandfather. Hundreds of questions I should have asked, but I didn't. I was young and stupid.

Don't think you know their story because you do not. Understand their hopes and fears, their struggles and accomplishments, their regrets or dreams. Know their story. And after they are gone, tell their stories, speak their names. And when you know their story, you will understand yours.

Linda

CHAPTER 5: RIVESVILLE—OUR TOWN

Even coming from small towns, the biggest dreams are possible.

Stephanie Labbe

We briefly pause to introduce a new character in our story: Rivesville. The town's warmth and sense of community were deeply intertwined with the immigrant experience. Rivesville significantly shaped the lives of our family members, and histories and memories of the town offer a vivid portrayal of close-knit neighbors, the vibrant spirit of the inhabitants, and the importance of local immigrant-owned retail stores. These stores represented ownership for many, including members of the Simonetti/Raspa family, and symbolized a particular status within the community and a means to support neighbors. Rivesville, along with its Italian American diaspora section Greentown, played a prominent and impactful role in the captivating story of Giorgio and Maria, both immediately after their arrival and later as they, along with their children, established Rivesville as their home.

Much of the details in this chapter come from Frank Spevock's excellent book, *Chimes of Time: A Local History*, which shows his memories of Greentown dating back to the 1930s.

Anita also shared her childhood memories of Greentown. Reflections and recollections of Rivesville during this era from others, including Frank Raspa's son Nick, who was interviewed for a feature story about Rivesville in the *Fairmont Times*, are also included. Let's start by taking a tour. (To assist with the tour, the numbers shown in parentheses correspond to the map later in of this chapter.)

Satterfield Street, where Giorgio and Maria ultimately lived, ran perpendicular to the Monongahela River, crossing over Clayton Street (the main street in town) and then passing Merril Avenue, which is on top of a very steep hill. As Anita stood on her parents' front porch facing Satterfield Street, if she turned right and walked up the street past the next road (Fear Street), she would reach the house on the corner of Fear and Satterfield, which belonged to the Spevock's (21). Anita mentioned that Jimmy Spevock was once her boyfriend. Directly across Satterfield Street from the Spevock's was the Detch house (spelling may be incorrect) (20). Their daughter was a friend of Anita's sister, Thresia. Anita recalled that Mrs. Detch and her neighbors, Mrs. Foresta and Mrs. Napolio, exhibited unusual behavior as they grew older. They would stand on their front porches and verbally harass people as they walked by on the street.

If Anita walked from her parent's house in the opposite direction, down Satterfield Street, and turned right onto Clayton Street, the first building on the corner was Koya's Grocery (4), later renamed Stanley's Store in the 1960s. Proceeding west, garages lined the right side of the road next to Koya's grocery. Beyond the garages, the new Catholic church (17), dedicated in 1950, stood on Kelly Street. The old Catholic church, built in the 1930s (18), was two streets behind the new one.

If Anita left home, turned left onto Satterfield Street and then left again onto Clayton Street, the first building she would have encountered was Chicky Joe's grocery store and bar (5). Chicky Joe was the nephew of Anita's Uncle Dominick Gearde, making him a cousin by marriage. His parents' home was on Fear Street, on the east end of the road that Maria's house was on. Later he purchased a large house on Fear Street, on the west side of Satterfield Street. Anita described it as a mansion and remembered that Chicky Joe also had a menacing goose that would chase passersby in the street.

Heading east on Clayton Street, the next building was Zukosky's Grocery Store (6). According to Spevock, Carl Zukosky ran a bustling grocery store next to Giorgio's shoe shop, offering a variety of small items. Anita recalls her father borrowing money from Mr. Zukosky for the shoe shop. As adults, Thresia, Carmella, and Ralphine each contributed fifty dollars monthly to Maria to help repay the loan.

[L] Frank at his father's shoe shop, circa 1946. [R] Anita Harbert and Lisa Hilt Healy (Frank's daughter) at the same shoe shop building, still standing but not operational, circa 1990. Family archives.

The next building was Giorgio's shoe shop (7). A 1935 calendar from the shop says, "Community Shoe Repair—George Simonetti." Over the years, the shoe shop was also called the Rivesville Shoe Hospital. Giorgio would go into Morgantown, West Virginia, a town about fifteen miles northeast of Rivesville, and buy supplies for his store from a store named Morgan Leather, or sometimes he would go into Fairmont, about five miles south, and buy supplies from the other shoemakers. Spevock describes Giorgio Simonetti as the "town's cobbler" and says, "He and his fine family lived just behind his shop. When it came to repairing shoes, he was tops!"

Continuing the tour east on Clayton Street, the next building was Dominick Munchin's Barber Shop (8), which was later moved one block over. Mrs. Oliverio owned a parcel near Munchin's Barber Shop, including a house and a garden. She was Anita's mother's friend and Anita's godmother, who sponsored her confirmation into the Church.

Raspa's State Theater. Movie playing:
Gladys Walton in Playing with Fire, circa 1921.
Family archives.

L-T. Frank and Raffaela Raspa. Notice
they are holding hands. Circa 1921.
Family Archives.

Inside the Raspa State Theater before seats were added, L-R: unknown, Raffaele
Raspa, unknown, unknown. Family Archives.

The next building was the State Theater (9), owned by Anita's uncles, Frank and Raffaele Raspa. Raffaele was listed as the proprietor of the State Theater at the time of his death in 1924. There was a narrow alley between the theater and Gearde's Store (10). Anita mentioned that the theater was required to have more than one exit, so a door inside the theater opened into that alley. The alley was the final stop for a child who could exit through a door in the back of Maria's house, walk a path past the neighboring apartments on the second floor of the theater building, and descend the wide cement steps into the alley to reach Gearde's Store (10) to buy candy. It felt like a secret passageway—so much fun. For a child, the alley was enchanting.

The State Theater was the pride of Greentown. Anita worked in the theater, sweeping and cleaning. When asked if she was paid, she replied no, but she got to watch movies for free.

The next building housed Angelina and Dominick Gearde's Store (10). Spevock wrote, "We had a nice little store on the right side of the State Theater, operated by kindly Mr. and Mrs. Dominick Gearde [*sic*], two of the sweetest people that ever lived!" Anita remembers her Aunt Angelina giving her popsicles whenever she visited the store.

The next building on the eastward tour down Clayton Street was Gahini's Store (11). The owners were from Hungary. The store was the go-to place for ice cream. To the east of Gahini's was Dolog's Beer Garden (12), where Anita remembers learning to play chopsticks on the piano. The Dolog's family home was close to the Simonetti home. Anita fondly recalls being "bosom buddies" with the Dolog's grandchildren, who had the last name Karus. She mentions that the Dolog home contained two apartments: one for the family and the other for their children and grandchildren.

Vegetable gardens were located behind all the buildings and homes on Clayton Street, stretching from Chicky Joe's Grocery Store to Dolog's Beer Garden. In an article by Goode in the *Fairmont Times*, Nick Raspa (Frank Raspa's son) recalled, "'When I was growing up, everyone had a garden. You saw no grass. Everyone put a garden in. They planted every vegetable you can think of,' Raspa said. 'People could also raise chickens and pigs within the city limits. And all around Rivesville, they had all kinds of fruit—apples, peaches, pears, blackberries, and pawpaws,' Raspa said. 'We were never out of fruit.'"

Next to Dolog's Beer Garden was a vacant lot that extended to the next street, Johnson. Anita remembers playing there with friends and sledding down Johnson Street in the winter. Across Johnson Street, on the same side, was Josephine Morrone's Store (13), owned by a friend of Anita's sister Thresia. Anita recalls that their school bus stop was at this corner. Also, here Anita remembers a few homes; one of them was where Josephine Morone lived.

Anita's recollection of Greentown continues. Behind Josephine Morrone's Store, as one ascended the hill toward Merrill Avenue, lay the entrance to a coal mine. Beyond Josephine Morrone's Store and the nearby houses, Clayton Street extended out of town to a mining community called Hites, named after R. M. Hite, who owned and operated coal mines in Rivesville and Kingmont.

The Dominick Foresta house (14) stood across Clayton Street from Gearde's Store. He was Rosa Benincasa's son from her first marriage. The family lived on the first and second floors and ran a beer garden in the basement. Across Clayton Street from the State Theater was Sophie Fisher's Store (15). Anita mentioned that Sophie sold soft drinks, hot dogs, and other items. She had a jukebox in the store, and Anita and her friends would go there to dance.

Frank Spevock recalled that area in 1935 as "a neat little 'Bachiee' court [*sic* Bocce] where guys would come after a day of work in the mines or on weekends." Bocce is an Italian game in which players roll balls toward a target ball, called the "pallino." It's also known as Italian lawn bowling.

Anita remembers the funny and descriptive names the locals gave to places they frequented. For example, there was a fruit stand across from Roger's Gas Station at the junction of Route 19 at the entrance to Greentown Hill. It was operated by a woman named Annie, so everyone in Greentown referred to her as "Annie Fruit Stand."

The Monongahela River was prominently featured in Rivesville. According to Spevock, Dayton Spencer operated a river ferry using several rowboats. Passengers from the villages on both sides of the river (Rivesville and a town across the river, Montana) rang a bell to summon the ferry. Anita remembers residents using a community rowboat to travel from Montana to Greentown for groceries. Additionally, showboats used to pass through and dock at Rivesville.

LEGEND

1. Giorgio & Maria's House
2. Beer Garden
3. Beer Garden
4. Koya's Grocery Store
5. Chicky Joe's Grocery Store
6. Zukoski/Roger's Grocery Store
7. Giorgio's Shoe Shop
8. Barber Shop
9. State Theater
10. Gearde's Store
11. Gahini's Grocery Store
12. Dolog's Beer Garden
13. Josephine Morrone's Store
14. Forrest House
15. Sofie Fisher's Store
16. Agelina's Hardware Store
17. New Catholic Church
18. Old Catholic Church
19. Chicky Joe's Mansion
20. Mrs. Detch's House
21. Spevock's House

Circa 1950s

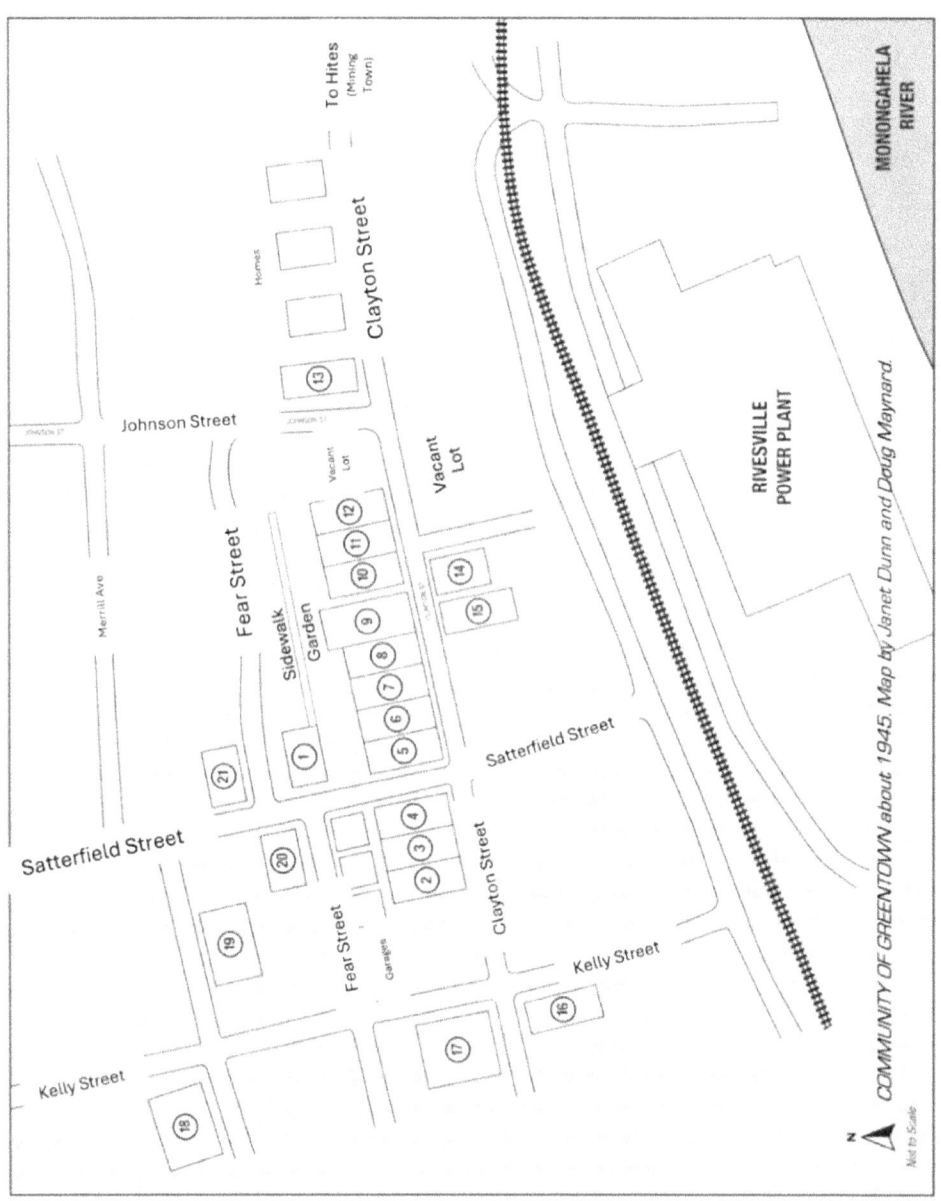

COMMUNITY OF GREENTOWN about 1945. Map by Janet Dunn and Doug Maynard.

Our tour of Rivesville isn't just about geography; it's also about capturing the town's essence. Goode quoted Nick Raspa in the *Fairmont Times* as he reminisced about the Rivesville of the past: "Everyone was so friendly. If you visited someone, they'd always have coffee and hard bread for you. Everyone made their own bread—it was delicious." Our Rivesville tour vividly showcases the heartbeat of the Italian American community. Exploring the town's history provides deeper insights into its origins and offers a richer perspective on the community that Giorgio and Maria selected for their American home.

The Making of Greentown/Rivesville

Rivesville is a small community located north of Fairmont and southwest of Morgantown (see map of Rivesville, West Virginia, later in this chapter). It sits on the banks of the Monongahela River, notably one of the few rivers in the world that flows north. The history of Rivesville begins with David Morgan, a soldier who served and surveyed alongside George Washington. Morgan had a farm on the Monongahela River near present-day Rivesville around 1779. His brother, Zackwell Morgan, bought land nearby and they established a settlement together. Their settlement, Pleasantville, and a nearby community, Paw Paw, were later combined and renamed Rivesville in honor of Rives Hoult, the father of some early settlers.

In 1919, Rivesville's central area was west of Route 19. It did not yet encompass Highlawns, which was located west of Rivesville, across Route 17 on Baxter Road. It also did not include Greentown, located east of Route 19. That year, a proposition on Rivesville's ballot asked voters whether the town should be expanded. The vote passed, but a few years later, when Greentown and Highlawns sought to separate from Rivesville, voters had to choose whether to keep Greentown and Highlawns as part of the town proper. Mayor J. W. Richards noted that if these communities disassociated from Rivesville, they could establish statutes that might not align with those of Rivesville. His examples included operating stores, playing baseball games, and watching movies on Sundays. Richards also argued that by including Greentown and Highlawns in the town, those areas could benefit from improvements and protections offered by the integration. The proposition to keep Greentown and Highlawns passed.

The town's population surged as coal mining expanded at the beginning of the twentieth century, creating a need for immigrants to fill the void. Still, immigrants arriving in the community of Rivesville may not have felt especially welcome. Their language and clothing were

Map of Rivesville and vicinity.

home lives, which set them apart from the locals. There were stories that some existing residents felt the darker-skinned Italian immigrants did not belong in their community. Italian immigrants throughout the United States faced discrimination and backlash in the early twentieth century. Most felt a stronger bond with fellow immigrants than with existing Americans. In Rivesville, Italians and others settled and lived outside the town, east of Route 19. Their immigrant community resembled a Little Italy typically found in larger cities, complete with shops and religious, social, and recreational places.

We don't know much about the relationship between the people of Rivesville (those living west of Route 19) and the folks from Greentown (which included coal miners and immigrants). However, we know that the lives of these different subcultures intertwined when their paths crossed in the daily activities of shopping, working, and recreation. Maria often walked from Greentown to the post office in Rivesville. Her children either took the bus or walked to the school all the children in town attended. People from Greentown bought supplies from the town's lumberyard and shopped at some of the retailers in Rivesville. Anita remembers seeing movies and shows at the theater in Rivesville. Some of Rivesville's residents visited Giorgio's shoe shop or caught films at the State Theater in Greentown.

Coal Mining

The first commercial coal mine opened in Rivesville in the early 1900s, almost one hundred years after West Virginia's first coal mine began operating in Wheeling. Rivesville had access to railroads and rivers, leading mining companies to establish operations in Rivesville and throughout the county. As a result of these mines, Rivesville's population increased ninefold from 190 in 1910 to 1,700 by 1930.

Coal mining was a way of life in Rivesville and throughout West Virginia. Coal companies sent recruiters to Italy and other countries to bring immigrants to the United States to work in the mines, answering the prayers of poor families with no future in economically struggling countries.

Because of the coal mines in Rivesville, work was available. Miners willingly descended deep underground for long, demanding, and dangerous hours to support their families. Early miners used rudimentary tools and equipment, while mining companies often neglected safety measures. Children as young as twelve and women also worked in the mines. It was a dirty and hazardous environment. Many on-the-job accidents resulted in numerous miners losing their lives, often due to methane gas explosions or mine collapses. Immigrants usually were assigned the most dangerous jobs. Many immigrant miners, as well as all miners, faced severe health issues later in life, such as black lung, because of exposure to coal dust.

Some of the coal mines around Rivesville were:

- The Parker Run Coal and Coke Company Mine operated from 1901 to 1913. Old newspaper articles sometimes called Greentown the Parker Run addition, named after the nearby Parker Run mine.
- The Consolidated Coal Company Mine No. 97 operated from 1922 to 1954. Its coal seam was located one hundred feet below the riverbed. In 1934, Consol. No. 97 employed 412 men, all members of the UMWA (United Mine Workers of America). The daily wage varied from $6.37 for loaders to $9.29 for cutters.
- The Virginia & Pittsburgh Coal & Coke Co.'s Morgan Mine No. 2 was a significant mining operation in Greentown. Its name came from the Morgan Mines, as it was part of the famous David Morgan Farm acreage at nearby Sugar Lane.

The local mining community was called Hites. For most of its history, the Hite family owned and operated the expansive Morgan mine, which was located a mile east of Rivesville. According to Spevock, the late Clyde J. Spiker, who managed the company store at Morgan Mines for many years, stated that mining began in 1910 and continued until June 14, 1951, when both the mine and the company store shut down permanently.

Coal mine owners did not pay workers in regular US currency. Instead, they compensated them with "miner's scrip." This scrip could only be used at stores owned by the coal mine, known as company stores. Prices at these coal company stores were much higher than those at community stores. Community stores that accepted scrip often added a markup to the goods purchased by miners. If a miner lacked enough scrip for their purchases, the company store would provide an "advance against unearned wages," resulting in predatory lending and a never-ending debt owed to the company store, which most families could never pay off. Miners had no choice but to work for scrip. According to Spevock, at the Hites company store, scrip money had the letter "H" punched into it. Since some miners' first language was not English, the company store displayed a derogatory sign at the pay window: *"No card, no scrip—No got, no get!"*

The coal companies also provided medical facilities for the miners and their families. The Hite mine had a doctor's office. The clinic once stitched up Anita's finger and treated Maria for a broken nose.

Maria was walking along the railroad tracks into Rivesville when she fell while heading to the post office to buy stamps. Still, with all these offerings, many workers dreamed of a time when they would not be in the mines, but few could escape its grip. Maria's brother, Frank Raspa, had his first job in the United States as a coal miner. His son Nick says that his father worked in the mines for about six months before deciding he needed to leave. He was one of the lucky ones who escaped.

The Famous Pepperoni Roll

Pepperoni Rolls may rank among the greatest inventions of the twentieth century. A coal miner named Giuseppe "Joseph" Argiro wanted a more convenient meal to carry in his miner's pail. He searched for something he could eat with one hand that wouldn't spoil, and that reminded him of home. Enter the Pepperoni Roll: a pocket-sized, soft white yeast bread roll with two pencil-sized sticks or multiple overlapping thin slices of pepperoni baked inside. Giuseppe's creation became so popular with the other miners that he left his job and opened the Country Club Bakery in Fairmont in 1927. The bakery still operates today. Pepperoni rolls are nearly impossible to find outside of West Virginia.

The Streetcar

The Daily Telegram in 1917 reported that the Monongahela Valley Traction Company "asks for the privilege of constructing a streetcar line

High streetcar trestle connecting Jasper Street with Rivesville over Paw Paw Creek. The picture was taken as it was being built in 1912. (Spevock, Chimes of the Time, 1981).

in the streets of the town, to erect poles, to operate cars, and other necessary things to carry on an electric car, a lighting and power service." The Rivesville Fairmont streetcar line ran alongside the lumber yard. Nick Raspa recalled that, during high school, kids would ride the streetcar into Fairmont for fun. Anita remembers when her father, Giorgio, and Uncle Frank took the streetcar to Fairmont for social meetings or to gather supplies.

Greentown had two streetcar stops: one at the first intersection on the right side of town and another further down the street on the same side, close to the Foreste home. The last Fairmont-Rivesville streetcar ran in 1947.

The Rivesville Power Plant

A man named "Toad" Satterfield operated a lumber mill along the banks of the Monongahela River in Greentown. We can assume that the lumber mill was still operating when Frank and Raffaele arrived in Greentown in 1913. This site eventually became the site of a massive power plant. We do not know whether Satterfield sold the land to Monongahela Power and the railway company or how it was acquired or selected. It was no doubt selected due to its proximity to the nearby coal mines, so it was a plus for the mines. We know the power plant site could not have been worse for the new immigrants and those living in the area. Their once-beautiful view of the river was forever changed by the monstrous plant that belched soot day and night.

Monongahela Power and the railway company built the Rivesville Power Plant. When construction started in 1917, Greentown was not part of the Rivesville corporation. There may not have been much concern for the immigrant families and coal miners living in the community. This narrative also reflects the story of low-income Americans who were always at risk. These immigrants were people outside Rivesville, lacking a voice or influence over the upcoming construction. They may have heard rumors from local coal miners or around town, but they likely had no say in what was being built. They could only watch and feel regret as the plant grew larger and potentially more toxic to their lives.

A camp was set up on-site for the workers building the plant. During the construction of the Rivesville Power Plant, the Monongahela Valley Traction Company added an extra streetcar to accommodate about one hundred men who commuted daily from Fairmont. The car left Fairmont at 6:15 a.m. and reached the construction site in Rivesville thirty minutes later. In the evening, a streetcar departed from the construction site at 5:15 p.m. to bring the workers back to Fairmont. The power plant was finished in mid-1919 and started operations while it was still under construction. It was so large that it blocked the river view for Greentown residents for almost three blocks.

Was Greentown Green?

At the beginning of the twentieth century, generating electricity from coal was a dirty and hazardous process that could have impacted the health of many residents in Rivesville. Giorgio and Maria's home was about one thousand feet from this massive power plant.

Coal was transported by barge or truck and dumped into the coal piles near the power station. It was then moved into large boilers using water sourced from the Monongahela River, producing steam to generate electricity. The boilers also may have emitted hazardous pollutants that were discharged from the plant's large stacks and then spread throughout the Rivesville community. Pollutants such as sulfuric and nitric acid, commonly called "acid rain," may have blanketed the small town. Many old photographs show minimal grass, few trees, and limited greenery, perhaps due to the acid rain. These pollutants could also have contaminated the Monongahela River, harming fish and other wildlife. At the peak of the plant's operation, there were few, if any, environmental regulations, especially when Maria and Giorgio lived nearby. To exacerbate the situation, on certain days the plant would "blow the stacks," an industrial high-pressure cleaning to prevent residue buildup inside the chimneys. Due to these volcanic-like eruptions, coal dust and soot would rain down and leave a couple of inches of black particulate matter on every house, street, and yard in the community.

There was no escaping Greentown's black soot. A recent post on the "Friends of Rivesville" Facebook page by William Scott Kosik, recalling the 1960s, stated, "If you were a kid and played outside in Greentown, you got soot dust all over you from the black coal smoke that came out of the power plant smokestack. All the Greentown kids looked like they came out of the coal mine." It was also deafeningly loud when the stacks blew. Another post, this one by Penny McGill, on that same page stated, "I always remember when the Power Plant let steam off from the stacks. As kids, we would scream and laugh as we couldn't hear ourselves (when it blew). I remember cleaning soot dust (not dirt) off my feet and dust off my clothes before entering the house."

Several members of Anita's family were diagnosed with cancer. Her father passed away from stomach and lung cancer. Her oldest sister had breast cancer, her brother had prostate cancer, and another sister had multiple myeloma, a relentless blood cancer. Even Anita herself was diagnosed with lung cancer. It's unknown if the nearby power plant caused or contributed to these or other health issues.

The State Theater

Frank Raspa, Maria's brother, returned home from serving in WWI in December 1918, intending to put on his grocer's apron and resume running his store. His sister, Angelina, had managed the store for him while he was away. Consequently, Angelina discovered that she enjoyed being a storekeeper, leading her and her husband, Dominick, to express their desire to keep the store.

In October 1920, Frank bought a parcel of land in Rivesville from D. W. Clayton and his wife for one thousand dollars. Frank and Raffaele's next venture involved building a theater on Clayton Street in Greentown. It is unclear how the brothers financed the construction, perhaps by negotiating with a movie production company to build the movie house. The following is an excerpt from an article on theater history: "Central to the [American film] industry's expansion was a strategy of buying and building movie theaters. By owning theater chains, the big producers ensured an outlet for their films. Producers could then confidently raise budgets for individual films."[3]

The Raspa brothers, Frank and Raffaele, constructed a theater with a capacity of five hundred seats and a stage. The installation of a large commercial movie projector made local headlines. In addition to movies, the brothers secured contracts for various live shows.

[3] "Theater Chains and the Structure of the Industry."

(L) Ticket from the State Theater in Greentown (R) Seats from the State Theater in Greentown that the authors found for sale in a nearby antique shop in 2024. Family archives.

The first movie shown at the State Theater by Frank and Raffaele, as proud co-owners, was *Wet Gold* in 1922. The State Theater was a single-screen venue. According to Nick Raspa, the State Theater primarily showcased westerns and adventure films and occasionally featured live "hillbilly music" and a magician named Jarvis. They used to have many family events there, like movies, boxing, stage shows, and even dance contests. A Facebook post on the Friends of Rivesville page from Maridate Hardesty states, "My grandmother, Kathleen 'Kitty' Hardesty, played the piano for the silent movies. She could rock a piano." Someone else on the Facebook page remembers the film *Legend of Tom Dooley*.

Nick Louis Fantasia, grandson of Giorgio and Maria and former mayor of Fairmont, explains that the State Theater in Rivesville was the immigrant theater for the Greentown community. There was another theater in Rivesville, the Rex Theater, that exclusively showed MGM films, while the State Theater only featured Warner Brothers films.

In 1941, Frank Raspa's eldest son, Ralph, became the manager of the State Theater. He cultivated a following for his movie reviews in *Box Office Magazine* and *The Motion Picture Herald*, which served small-town movie exhibitors. He and his brothers, Nick and Sam, were experts in movie trivia.

Anita recalls that the theater had double features. She once fell asleep between shows, hit her head, and needed stitches. The theater closed in 1960 and remained vacant until it was destroyed by fire on August 13, 2004.

Our Town, the American classic by Thornton Wilder, is a play about the people's lives in the fictional small town of Grover's Corners, New Hampshire, from 1901 to 1913. The play centers on two families, the Webbs and the Gibbs, and their children, Emily Webb and George Gibbs, who fall in love, marry, and experience both happiness and tragedy. The three acts of the play are titled "Daily Life," "Love and Marriage," and "Death and Eternity." In the play's final moments, Emily is allowed to revisit a day in her life, and she realizes that she never fully appreciated what she had until it was gone.

Greentown is *our town*. The family names in our story, Simonetti and Raspa, have more vowels than those in the famous play. Anita is our Emily. The story of this place is as fundamental as any aspect of Giorgio and Maria's story. Great narratives span many genres, including tragedies, comedies, thrillers, musicals, sci-fi, and even fantasies, but the genre of our Rivesville story is none of these. The tale of Rivesville, flaws and all, is a love story.

Giorgio and Maria traveled over land and sea to reach Rivesville. They faced numerous hardships and indignities before and after arriving in the United States. The Statue of Liberty, welcoming them to New York Harbor with the inscription "Give me your tired, your poor, Your huddled masses yearning to breathe free, The wretched refuse of your teeming shore," did not mention what would come after immigrants landed in America. Giorgio and Maria's life in America started in their newly adopted community of Rivesville, West Virginia.

They were fortunate. They had each other and a loving extended family waiting for them. They also had this place, this enclave that was part Italy and part America, which offered a glimpse of the past, inseparable from the promise of the future. What better starting point could they ask for? Against the backdrop of the mountainous horizon, the cool blue waters of the Monongahela, and the embrace of hope, things were looking up for the first time in a long while.

* * *

It was time to make their home in Rivesville and get America to live up to its promise.

Dear Aunt Nita,

In researching and writing a chapter about when Maria and Giorgio, my grandmother and grandfather, came to Rivesville, I have all sorts of sad feelings for them about leaving their homeland and family. How they subjected themselves (and Rosa) to the weeks of traveling on the ocean, then to West Virginia in December and January! I read about the conditions that the immigrants had to put up with on the ship and more about the prejudice and bigotry toward Italians after they arrived in America. My heart just aches for them.

I was writing about how West Virginia looks like Southern Italy, where we visited, and how maybe Rivesville reminded them a little of home. I am sad and angry that the powers-that-be built that power station where they did and took away Greentown's view and access to the river. Their actions made Greentown dirty and even perhaps infested with unknown diseases and illnesses.

And I am sad that there wasn't the technology for Giorgio to have a Zoom call with his mom before he died. She survived the ravages of WWII with only one hope: to see her son again. It was not to be.

Then I decided to print off your resume and read through it. First, I cried. I'm still crying. Your folks would have been so very, very proud of you. Each of their children had gifts and talents that helped make their communities a better place, but what you have accomplished has influenced our country and our world.

God tells us that we don't always see the results of our actions in our lifetime, like Abraham and Moses. Maria and Giorgio didn't. I am very proud that their sweet little soot-covered Italian daughter impacted many lives worldwide, especially the underprivileged among us. It helps even the score a little.

Thank you for sharing your life with us. Thank you for being one amazing lady. Thank you for being our second mom.

I love you!

Janet

Mor... *...orge Simonet...*
...OX 506

CATANZARO
MILITARY CENSORSHIP
NEW YORK N.Y. C.P.D.
DUE 10 CENTS

...zia ne avret...
...o forza ma
...ma non
...sola senza
...nti spiegatem...
...o zio, perchè qui
...no quando si ha
...coi lui?

cugina
Simonetti Vittoria

Launaro 10-3-945
Fotografia - Rip. vietata

...icca Carmine
Roma 20 Incis.
Cosenza
(Italia)

Alla cara picco...
Annita Luisa
RIVESVILLE SHOE HOSPITAL
GIORGIO SIMONETTI, PROP...
P.O. BOX 106
RIVESVILLE, W. VA

CATANZARO 14-3-45 CORR...

...appen...
...manna, allora
...fila ed è venut...
mostrandomi quello di...

CHAPTER 6: PASTA & MAGIC
1921–1946

Life is a combination of pasta and magic.

Federico Fellini

The nearly twenty years from 1921 to 1946 marked a period of growth for the Raspa and Simonetti families, both personally and professionally. If their journey to America was the antipasti course of their lives, these following decades symbolize the *primi piatti*, their first course. This course, filled with pasta and magic, was rich in experiences and best understood in the order it was served, year by year, until the magic faded.

The pioneering Raspa siblings—excluding Isabella, who remained behind—arrived in America between 1907 and 1913 and settled into their new lives in Rivesville. By the time Giorgio, Maria, and her mother arrived in 1921, the Raspa family was thriving, having established new businesses, friendships, and families. Greentown welcomed the Simonetti and Raspa families and many other immigrants seeking a better life. These newcomers shared a fundamental aspiration: to find acceptance in the new land they had risked everything to reach. Families that had made the journey before them warmly welcomed these immigrants, just as they, a few months or years earlier, had also been welcomed after they, too, had taken such risks to come to Rivesville.

We don't know why Giorgio's family didn't emigrate as well. Out of character to Italy's paternalistic society, Giorgio followed Maria's family. This suggests that the families were well acquainted in Italy and that Giorgio felt comfortable with the Raspas. We even speculate that Giorgio and Maria married before moving to the United States. One cannot look at the sole photo we have of them in Italy without imagining it was a wedding photo. That speculation is sensible for several reasons. As the introduction describes, the image is striking due to their attire and closeness. Additionally, being already married and familiar with the Raspa family provides context for Giorgio leaving his family behind to live with Maria. He was already part of their family.

Giorgio and Maria's long journey was nearing its end. After departing from the Fairmont, West Virginia train station, located roughly five miles north of Rivesville along the Monongahela River, they finally arrived at and entered the small town of Rivesville. As they arrived, Giorgio, Maria, and Rosa passed several businesses and homes on Main Street, which ran alongside the river. Then the road turned to the left and the town faded from view. They traveled a short distance before making a sharp right turn and ascending a steep hill. In the years to come, this slope would be known as Greentown Hill, a beloved spot among the community's children for sledding.

This old postcard might be a clue to what Giorgio and Maria saw as they arrived on Main Street in Rivesville in 1921. Public domain.

As the car climbed the hill, they may have spotted Rivesville High School at the intersection. They dreamed of having children who would one day attend that school. They hoped their children would receive a quality education in this new land and have opportunities they never had in Italy. Filled with optimism for the future, they wished for their children to grow into successful second-generation Italian Americans.

In 2016, when we traveled to Italy to visit Catanzaro, Stilo, and Petilia Policastro, where Giorgio and Maria had once lived. we saw rocky hills and green valleys that sloped down to the still-blue Tyrrhenian Sea. When Giorgio and Maria saw the mountains of West Virginia and the tranquil waters of the Monongahela River, it likely reminded them of their home across the ocean. Happy to be at the journey's end, Giorgio might have pulled Maria close and begun to sing.

The community of Greentown went about their daily business. Perhaps some residents would have paused their work upon hearing Giorgio's rich tenor voice in the distance. Giorgio, Maria, and Rosa reached the top of the hill leading into Greentown and caught sight of their new home for the first time.

As they moved deeper into the small town, Giorgio and Maria likely concentrated on looking for familiar faces. However, their attention was probably soon drawn to the right as they reached the town center. They may have been surprised by the enormous size of the massive power plant on the riverbank below Greentown.

That day, the focus was not on the scenery but on the homecoming. How happy the travelers must have been! What joy they must have felt upon hearing the melodic lilt of the Italian language from those welcoming them to their new home. It's likely that all their weariness simply vanished. They were finally home! Maria and Rosa had not seen Angelina for almost ten years and Frank and Ralph for over seven years. Rosalie probably lived in Detroit at that time, so she might have missed this joyful reunion. Family is important to Italians, and this day was surely filled with singing, dancing, food, and laughter.

The official American marriage certificate, below, for Giorgio and Maria states that they were married in Marion County (where Rivesville is located), West Virginia, on January 20, 1921. They may have also married before they left Italy. At that time, there were two types of marriage ceremonies in Italy. The first was a civil ceremony, somewhat comparable to obtaining a marriage license in the United States. If the couple participated in a civil marriage ceremony in Italy, they were legally married. The second type of marriage ceremony was a religious ceremony held in the church.

Authority.

Clerk's Certificate.

Preliminary Inquiries and Answers Thereto, Made and ascertained by A. M. MARTIN, Clerk of the County Court of Marion County, State of West Virginia, relative to Mr

of County and State of

and M of Marion County and State of West Virginia

to whom the accompanying Marriage License is issued.

The Full Names of the Parties are as Follows:

His full name is Her full name is

His age is 26 Her age is

He was born in County, State of

She was born in County, State of

His place of residence is

Her place of residence is Marion County

The name of the party giving the foregoing information is

of County, State of

Given under my hand this 20th day of 1921

Clerk County Court

Marriage License.

West Virginia, County of Marion, to-wit:

To any person licensed to celebrate Marriage:

You are hereby authorized to join together, in the Holy State of Matrimony, according to the Rites and Ceremonies of your church, or religious denomination, and laws of the State of West Virginia,

and

Given under my hand, as Clerk of the County Court of the County of Marion, this 20th

day of 192

Clerk

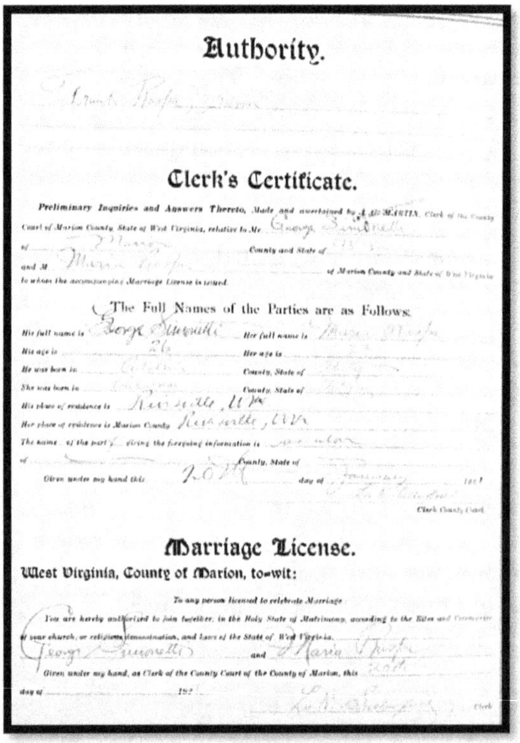

*L–R: Angelina, Maria, Giorgio. Child unknown, circa 1921.
Family archives.*

The picture of Giorgio and Maria with Angelina, above, might be their first photograph together in America. Maria appears to be pregnant with Thresia. They look young, strong, and at the peak of their new lives.

Giorgio initially worked in the coal mine but found it too dirty for his liking. He then opened his shoe shop in Greentown, likely with Aria, his favorite cobbler's hammer, by his side. An old, undated photo (next page) shows the inside of Giorgio's shoe shop.

Maria and Giorgio in the shoe shop. Family archives.

L-R: Giorgio, unknown, Frank Raspa.

Note the town in the background and the state of the structures. Notice Giorgio's watch chain and watch, which we saw in his wedding picture in Italy. Family archives.

An old photograph of the grocery store (below), built by Frank Raspa, reveals that the building housed two businesses. The left side of the window is labeled "F. Raspa, Grocer," while the right is marked "Shoe Shop."

*Frank Raspa's Grocery Store on the bottom left
with Giorgio's Shoe Shop on the bottom right. Angelina and Dominick Gearde are on the top
porch while their son/stepson is on the bottom porch. Family archives*

Greentown was expanding, yet it remained a mining town. By to-day's standards, it could be considered little more than a shantytown, with muddy streets and dilapidated houses. However, for those who lived there, it was home and represented the fulfillment of the dreams they had fought to achieve.

Thresia

Giorgio and Maria initially lived in one of the apartments above the the store. Their first child, Thresia Christine Simonetti, was born on September 23, 1921. She was likely named after Giorgio's mother, Teresa DeLuca. Thresia Simonetti was such a beautiful child that a neighbor, who was incredibly jealous of Giorgio and Maria's lovely daughter, actually tried to harm the little girl. Thresia grew up to be a stunningly beautiful woman with Hollywood looks, but as far as we know, this was the only time anyone wanted to harm her for being beautiful.

Carmella

Carmella Delores Simonetti was born on November 8, 1922. She was Giorgio and Maria's second child and their second daughter. She was likely named after Giorgio's father, Dominico Carmelo Simonetti. The following year, Nicola (Nick) Fantasia was born on January 3, 1923, in Kingmont, West Virginia. He was the son of Luzio Fantasia and Rose DiGiacomo Fantasia, who lived a few doors down from Mary Guzzo.

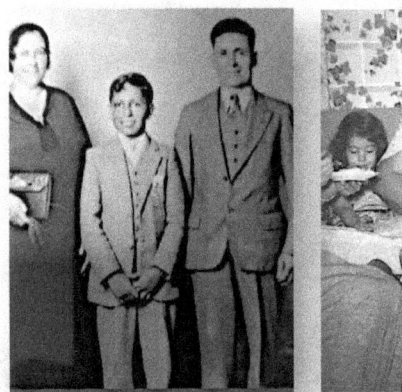 

[L] Rose, Nick, and Luzio Fantasia.
[R] Georgiana [Carmella's daughter], Rose, and Maria. Family archives.

Mary was Maria's best friend, although the circumstances of Maria and Mary's meeting are unknown. Mary Guzzo lived just south of Fairmont in Kingmont, a community similar to Greentown and about eight miles south of Rivesville along the river. Many Italian American immigrants lived and worked in the mines in Kingmont. Maria would take her children to visit Mary, who lived in one of the coal mining "company houses." Mary and Maria were such good friends that Maria became the godmother of Mary's children, and Mary became the godmother of Maria's children. The friendship was fortuitous as Carmella and Nick would later marry.

Raffaele

Maria's brother, Raffaele Raspa, became a naturalized citizen in 1922. The process started on November 3, 1919. The form he submitted indicates that he was twenty-four years old. It notes he had a dark complexion, stood at 5'5" tall, and had black hair and brown eyes. It also mentions that he was missing his right hand's first and little fingers. The form states that he traveled from Naples to New York on the S.S. San Giovanni, that he hailed from Petilia Policastro, Italy, and that he currently lived in the United States. It indicates that he was unmarried, worked as a merchant, and had to renounce all allegiance and fidelity to any foreign prince, potentate, state, or sovereignty forever, particularly Victor Emanuel III, king of Italy. The form he signed also declared, "I am not an anarchist; I am not a polygamist, nor a believer in the practice of polygamy; and it is my intention in good faith to become a citizen of the United States of America and to permanently reside therein. So help me, God." Raffaele submitted a Petition for Naturalization on February 17, 1922. This form contained much of the same information, along with details like his ability to speak English and the fact that he had resided in the United States of America for five years immediately preceding the date of the petition.

Raffaele Raspa married Mary Clara Rucci (b. 1907) around 1922. Mary was about fifteen years old when they married, while Raffaele was approximately twenty-eight. Their son, Nicolas (Nikolas) Ralph Raspa, was born in Marion County on August 15, 1923. Giorgio and Maria had nieces and nephews in Italy, as Maria's sister Isabella and

Giorgio's siblings still lived there. However, Nicolas would be Maria's and Giorgio's first nephew in Greentown, here in America. Everything appeared to be going as planned, with the Simonetti/Raspa families growing and prospering.

Then, suddenly, tragedy struck. Raffaele Raspa, the youngest of the Raspa brothers, sadly passed away in Rivesville, West Virginia, on April 28, 1924, at the age of twenty-nine. His death certificate indicated that the cause of death was cardiac disease due to cardiac dropsy.

The picture below was taken at the cemetery, showing an open casket. Behind them on the hill are members of a band in uniform holding instruments. In American society today, this photograph may seem a bit macabre because of the open casket. The approximate count of attendees was over one hundred. They were mainly from the close-knit community of Greentown. Maria is six months pregnant with her third child, and Giorgio is shown in one of the rare pictures of him without a hat, no doubt out of respect for the solemn occasion.

Burial of Raffaele Raspa, April 1924.
1. Dominick Gearde, 2. Angelina Raspa Gearde, 3. Maria Raspa Simonetti,
4. Rosalie Raspa Gelfo, 5. John Gelfo, 6. Mary "Clara" Raspa,
7. Rosa Benincasa, 8. Frank Raspa. 9. Giorgio Simonetti. Family archives.

In the cemetery, on a tall column marking the young man's grave, there is a picture of Maria's handsome brother who was only three years older than she. The inscription on his column reads "Riposano le passe (rest in peace) di Raffaele Raspa nato (born) 18 December 1894, Petilia Policastro, Prov Catanzaro, mort (died) in Rivesville 28 April 1924." The bottom of the stone reads "He was the sunshine of our home, and now he's gone but not forgotten." What stood out to us when we visited his grave in 2024 was that he was buried alone in the back of the cemetery; later, all his relatives were buried in an adjoining cemetery. Nonetheless, his generation did not forget him, but the next generations did, until now. Rest in peace, Great Uncle Raffaele.

Ralphine

Three months after Raffaele's death, Maria and Giorgio welcomed their third daughter, named after Maria's recently deceased brother, Raffaele. Raffaelina Simonetti, nicknamed Ralphine, born on July 19, 1924. The same year Ralphine was born, Lewis Dean Tennant, the son of Charlie and Ida Tennant, was born just a few miles from Rivesville on April 27, 1924. They would later marry.

Growing up, we often heard stories about Ralphine being a tomboy. One popular tale recounted how Ralphine, as a young girl, "beat up" her cousin George "Chicky Joe" Gearde. Chicky Joe was a schoolmate and the nephew of Dominick Gearde, who married Maria's sister, Angelina. We know we shouldn't applaud violence, but it's one of those family stories that has persisted, with a chuckle, as a testament to Ralphine's verve.

Ralphine was a mischievous child full of life and innocent practical jokes. In that long-ago era when a light swat on the bottom was acceptable as a form of light discipline, Maria tried to discipline Ralphine for something long forgotten. Ralphine, still a young but willful child, took her punishment without tears or shame. Maria was so fraught by Ralphine's lack of reaction that she yelled down the road to the shoe shop for Giorgio to come home, pleading, "Ralphine won't cry! Ralphine won't cry!"

Marriage, Naturalization, and Daughters

In May 1925, Francesco (Frank) Simonetti, Maria's only living brother, married Catherine "Catrina" Scalisa, also known by the Americanization of her name, Scolish, in Taylor County, West Virginia. Catherine was eighteen years old, while Frank was thirty-three. She was born in Berryburg, West Virginia, and lived in Barbour County. Raffaele's wife, Mary Rucci, also hailed from Berryburg, West Virginia, and both she and Catherine were born around 1907. They may have been friends or schoolmates.

On July 30, 1926, Giorgio petitioned for naturalization with the Department of Labor Naturalization Service. Naturalization was a two-step process that took at least five years. After residing in the United States for two years, an immigrant could file a "declaration of intention" (first papers) to become a citizen. After three more years, the immigrant could "petition for naturalization" (second papers). Once the petition was granted, a certificate of citizenship was issued to the new citizen. We found no documentation indicating that Maria petitioned for naturalization alongside Giorgio. However, we do know that by 1950 Maria was listed as naturalized in the census.

Giorgio and Maria's three daughters—Thresia, Carmella, and Ralphine—were growing up and developing their unique personalities. From all signs, Giorgio's shoe shop was thriving. We can only assume that the only thing missing for Giorgio and Maria was a son.

(L) Thresia, Frank, Ralphine, and Carmella, circa 1928. (R) Frank, date unknown. Family archive.

Frank, Finally!

Praise God, Giorgio and Maria's first and only son, Frank Dominick Simonetti, arrived on August 15, 1928. Frank's middle name, Dominick, was probably after Giorgio's father, Dominico Carmelo Simonetti. We can only imagine Giorgio and Maria's joy. We will not assume that Frank was spoiled as the only boy, but Mama Mia, he must have had a wonderful childhood. The sisters may have been indifferent about having a brother with one crucial exception: when they played house, they made Frank play the husband, hence his lifelong nickname, "Hubby."

First Row: Ralphine. Second Row L-R: Giorgio, Frank, Carmella, Thresia, Maria. Circa 1929. Family archives.

390 Satterfield Street

[Left] Giorgio and Maria's house at 390 Satterfield Street. Front of the house faces Satterfield Street. [Right] Front of the house with Ralphine (L) and Thresia (R) dressed in costume. Family archives.

Before Frank's birth, the family lived in an apartment on Clayton Street, over the store that the Raspa family owned. When Frank was born, Giorgio and Maria bought a house at 390 Satterfield Street.

The house may have once been a store before it was transformed into a home. Giorgio and Maria hired someone to install walls inside the structure. It was a small home, about 1,200 sq. ft. Even with the remodel, it had some unusual features for a residence. Firstly, there were two front doors. If you entered through the left door after ascending the stairs, you would find yourself in the living room. Using the door that was straight ahead after ascending the stairs led to one of the two bedrooms. As a result, this door remained locked and was never used as an entrance. Secondly, the house didn't have hallways; every room was connected to the next. Lastly, the layout was unconventional. For example, the bathroom was accessed by walking through the dining room. These are all possibly indications that the building was originally a store that the Simonetti family remade into a house. The house featured an apartment on the second floor.

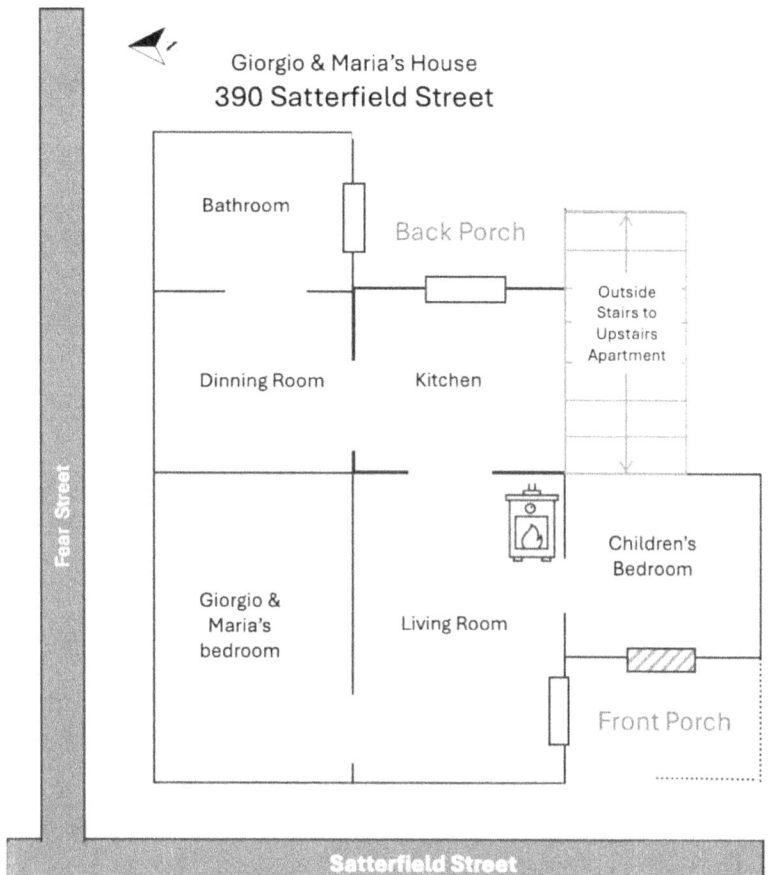

Giorgio & Maria's House
390 Satterfield Street

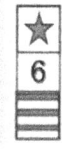

There was also a shanty, or small separate living space, in the back-yard. An outhouse was situated in the backyard between the house and the shanty. Later, bathrooms were added inside the house, up-stairs apartment, and the shanty. Part of the back porch was sacrificed to accommodate the main floor bathroom.

Across from the front door, as you entered the living room, was a sofa against the far wall. Over the sofa were several pictures of Giorgio as a young man. There was an oversized Naugahyde chair and a light on the right wall of the living room beyond the children's bedroom door. Beside it sat a coal-burning potbellied stove. Maria sat there, crocheting as she visited with the people. Her hands flew! With the tiniest crochet hook, she created beautiful bedspreads. Behind the front door was a tall radio/record player, with its many 78 RPM records that Giorgio listened to, many of which were operas in Italian.

In 2025, Nancy, Diane, and their cousin Nick Fantasia rescued over one hundred fifty shellac 78 RPM records from Carmella and Ralphine's family homes that belonged to Giorgio. Most are from the 1920s and 30s. In one of the boxes with the records, we found Giorgio's subscription to the Metropolitan Opera for purchasing records. We also found Giorgio's shoe store checkbook in the box; with many checks he had written still inside. The checkbook balance was $37.36. Nancy meticulously cleaned and cataloged them. She purchased a turntable that played 78s and was thrilled to listen to them after they sat dormant in attics for over eighty years. She later digitized the ones in the best condition so present and future family members might know Giorgio and Maria through their "playlist."

If you turned right after entering the front door, you would find a small bedroom where all the children slept. There was a double bed for the three girls and a single cot in front of the blocked second front door for Frank. As the girls got older, Frank moved to the couch in the living room. When Anita came along, she slept in a crib in Giorgio and Maria's bedroom.

If you walked straight through the living room, you would enter the kitchen at the back of the house. It had a small table and a few chairs. Maria was a fantastic cook. Spaghetti sauce simmered all day with beef bones, chicken legs, and thighs. Money was tight, so she would go to the butcher and buy the cheapest cuts of meat. When the neighbors butchered, she would make blood pudding out of fresh pigs' blood and Hershey® bars. She canned and stored the "pudding" in the basement alongside other canned goods, including hot peppers in tomato sauce and an Italian ratatouille made with zucchini, onions, tomatoes, and vegetables they grew in their garden. Most locals from Southern Italy grew several unique types of hot peppers from seeds they had brought with them from the old country. For Southern Italians, hot peppers were serious business. Maria also baked cookies and treats for everyone. Her fried bread dough was the best! Maria would roll the warm fried dough in sugar. It was indescribably delicious.

MARIA'S ITALIAN LOVE KNOTS

1 doz. Eggs
1 1/2 c. Sugar
1 lb. Shortening
1 t. Vanilla

6 t. Baking Powder
6 c. Flour (more if needed)

Cream sugar and shortening. Add eggs, vanilla, baking powder, and flour. Roll dough into strips and tie into knots. Place on greased cookie sheet and bake at 350° for 12 minutes. Ice and add sprinkles.

MARIA'S CHOCOLATE OIL CAKE

3 c. Flour
2 c. Sugar
6 T. Cocoa Powder
2 t. Baking Soda
1 t. Salt

2/3 c. Oil
2 T. Vinegar
1 1/2 T. Vanilla
2 c. Water

Mix all together, adding water last. Bake at 300° for 50 min., or until done. Icing optional.

RASPA PITZALLAS
(PIZZELLES)

1 lb. Butter
2 c. White Sugar
2 1/2 c. Brown Sugar
8 c. Flour

1 doz. Eggs
1 T. Orange Extract
1 T. Baking Powder

--or add enough flour until not sticky. Drop spoon sized mounds onto pizzelle iron and bake until desired doneness.

EASTER BREAD

23 C. FLOUR
1 C. MELTED CRISCO
3 C. SUGAR
1 C. BROWN SUGAR
1/2 LARGE CAKE YEAST
12 EGGS
1/2 BOTTLE LEMON EXTRACT
3 DROPS YELLOW FOOD COLORING
4 CUPS WATER, OR ENOUGH TO MIX

KNEAD UNTIL THOROUGHLY MIXED. ADD A LITLE OIL WHEN WORKING TO KEEP FROM STICKING. LET RISE ONE TIME. DO NOT PUNCH DOUGH DOWN. PUT IN PAN. BAKE AT 300 DEGREES. YOU HAVE TO WATCH SO IT WON'T BURN. COOL.

NOTE: When Maria made this she braided it around Easter colored eggs. Maria did not have written recipes. This version was told to her daughter, who told it to her daughter, etc. until it was finally written down. Some things were lost in translation!

Maria's artistry and skill are on display. Her recipes were not written, and many have been lost to time. At the bottom is just one example of her incredible skill as a crocheter. She was so fast and adept that she moved like a machine. She crocheted and watched TV or talked, never looking at her work and never dropping a stitch. Her creations live on and are true works of art.

Walking directly through the kitchen led to a back door and onto a covered porch. Maria prepared two hot meals each day without fail. When dinner was ready, she stepped out onto the back porch and whistled like one might call a cab in NYC. Her whistle was loud and clear, and meant for only one person. Giorgio would hear the whistle, close the shoe shop, and head home for dinner.

In the dining room, family photos from Italy, the old country, hung on the wall in large, heavy oval frames. The subjects in the photos wore ominous expressions; none smiled. The tone of the pictures was reminiscent of film noir. They were scary and intimidating to us kids.

Additionally, Maria kept a steamer trunk in the dining room. This came from Italy on the ship with Giorgio and Maria. Inside, the top tray was always filled with pizzelles, the famous Italian cookie that resembles lace and is made using a pizzelle press. Opening that trunk was like discovering treasure for a kid; it more than compensated for the intimidating pictures on the wall. Underneath the trunk was a trap door that led to the dark, damp cellar. There was also an outside door to the cellar on the side of the house, but when the weather was bad and Maria needed something from the cellar, she would ask Anita to retrieve it by using the trap door. Anita did so with reluctance.

On the far side of the dining room was the only bathroom. It contained a small sink, a tub, a toilet, and a ringer washer. Maria dried the clothes outside on a line that stretched across the back porch. The stairs to the upstairs apartment were on the opposite side of the back porch bathroom. One idea that Giorgio and Maria had for the future was to connect the upstairs apartment with the downstairs living area, but that idea never came to fruition. Another plan was that the upstairs apartment and the shanty in the back would provide Giorgio and Maria with some extra income. That plan, as we will see, infrequently succeeded.

The odd second door on the front porch was eventually bricked up, and a high window was added, replacing the puzzle of the house's entry. The porch underwent some refurbishing, removing the wooden balusters and adding a block wall and new balusters. Later, a sidewalk was constructed from the street to the front porch steps. Eventually, a tall hedge encircled the postage-stamp front yard, with openings at the sidewalk leading to the front porch and at a corner connecting to the narrow side yard.

The house at 390 Satterfield must have answered Giorgio and Maria's prayers. After eighteen years of saving, they finally had enough money to buy the home, which became the centerpiece of their lives. It was small, modest, and a tight fit for seven people, but it belonged to them. It was the only home they ever knew.

In the era of Giorgio and Maria, Greentown was a wonderful place to grow up. The Raspa and Simonetti families played a crucial role in the business community, encompassing the store, the theater, and the shoe shop. Frank Spevock mentioned that everyone was poor during his childhood in Greentown, yet no one seemed to notice. They grew much of their own food and tended to their gardens. They had everything they needed and supported each other whenever possible. They worked, attended church, shared meals, swapped stories, and fostered a community of love and hope.

Imagine finally settling down and having everything going in the right direction, only for the world to come crashing down around you. In 1929 the Great Depression struck, and Giorgio and Maria's generation would never be the same. The impact of the Depression was etched into their lives forever.

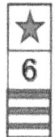

Many Italian Americans faced challenges finding work even before the Great Depression and endured widespread discrimination. The situation became significantly more difficult during the Depression, impacting them even more than others in America. They were met with a surge of intense prejudice and nativist hostility. Just as today, there was considerable anti-immigrant sentiment in the 1920s and 1930s. Unfortunately, the situation deteriorated with the onset of the Great Depression, during which immigrants—mainly Irish and Italian—were scapegoated for taking American jobs. Simultaneously, the media spread bigoted theories, advancing pseudo-scientific notions suggesting that "Mediterranean" types were inherently inferior to those of Northern European descent. Caricatures and songs depicting new immigrants as childlike, criminal, or subhuman became disturbingly commonplace. Anti-immigrant organizations emerged across the nation, and the Ku Klux Klan experienced a rise in membership. Catholic churches and charities endured vandalism and arson while mobs targeted Italians. In one year alone, more than twenty Italians were lynched. Anti-immigrant sentiment persisted into the late 1920s, culminating in the US Congress imposing strict immigration restrictions. The passage of this legislation marked the end of the significant era of Italian immigration.

It's possible that the small enclave of Greentown isolated Maria, Giorgio, and their family from the widespread discrimination faced by many Italian Americans throughout the United States, but that's probably not the case. They had to engage with society and interact with many citizens who did not want them in their community. We don't know of specific incidents or wrongdoings they encountered, and we can only speculate that it must have been difficult, especially when the Depression struck.

The Simonetti/Raspa clan were small business owners whose businesses heavily relied on the prosperity of the coal companies. During the Great Depression, coal miners in West Virginia faced significant hardships. With decreased demand, the coal industry experienced a steep decline, resulting in widespread job losses across the region. Italian miners were often the first to lose their jobs during this time. Laid-off miners no longer had to buy boots from Giorgio or groceries from Frank. It must have been a tough time for everyone in Greentown and America. As with every other hardship they faced, Giorgio and Maria persevered.

The United States Census takes place every ten years. In 1930, workers were hired to visit each home and interview the heads of households. Due to the language barrier, census workers often spelled family names according to how they were pronounced. The 1930 census provided the following information:

George Simonetti lives with his wife Mary and their 4 children – Tresa (Thresia age 8), Carmelo (Carmella age 7), Raffelina (Raffaelina) (age 5), Frank (age 1). Shoe Cobbler. He owns his own home on Satterfield Street, valued at $3,700, immigration dates are 1920. George is naturalized. Maria is listed as alien. Language spoken is "Italian" and George is not listed as a veteran.

Frank Raspa owns his own home on Clayton Street, valued at $5,000. 32 years old and married. Can read and write, finished the 6th grade. Is naturalized and speaks English. Lives with his wife and sons Ralph (age 3), Nick (age 1), and Sam (age 0). Industry: picture show, class of work, working on own account. Living with them is Rosa Raspa—mother. Rosa is listed as an alien who is unable to speak English.

Meanwhile, the Simonetti children started school. It surprised the school administrators that neither Carmella nor Ralphine could speak English. We don't know how Thresia slipped by, but she was unaffected. Carmella and Ralphine may have picked up some English in the community. Still, their language and writing skills were insufficient, causing them to be held back for one or two years and graduate with students younger than themselves.

Meanwhile, we learned that Giorgio may have had visions of a musical career. We don't have exact details, but we've heard stories about Giorgio's beautiful tenor voice and his love for opera. During the late 1930s, he had the chance to sing on a local station in Fairmont, WMMN. We don't know how it happened, how often he performed, or who accompanied him. Unfortunately, we never got to hear Giorgio's beautiful tenor voice ourselves. We were told he sang the great songs of Caruso, songs of everyday life elevated through opera. The ordinary was made extraordinary.

Anita, Surprise!

An unexpected arrival occurred while the older Simonetti siblings were in high school. Surprise! Anita Louise Simonetti, the fifth and youngest child of Maria and Giorgio, was born on March 4, 1937, when Maria was forty. Thresia, about sixteen, felt quite embarrassed that her mother was pregnant. To assuage their daughters, Maria told them they could name the baby, and they chose Anita after actress Anita Louise.

(L) Maria, Anita, and Carmella. circa. 1937.
(R) Giorgio and Anita. Circa 1942.
Family archives.

Rosa

Also in 1937, Rosa Benincasa, Maria's mother, passed away on June 13 in Rivesville. Rosa was strong and courageous. At sixty-three she had journeyed on a ship with Maria and Giorgio across the ocean. Before coming to the United States, her occupation was listed as "spinner" in Italian documents. She married her first husband, Giuseppe Foreste, in Italy, and they had a son, Dominick, who moved to the United States. Rosa stayed in Italy and, after Giuseppe's death, she married a miner named Nicola Raspa. In Petilia Policastro, Italy, she gave birth to children Isabella, Angelina, Rosalie, Francesco, Raffaele, and Maria. Nicola passed away around 1907. Maria, the youngest, was just ten years old when her father died, foreshadowing the challenges ahead for Anita.

As an old woman, Rosa lived in an apartment above the theater in Greentown, surrounded by her loving family. Neighborhood children would knock on her door to play a game with her, and she would playfully tease them by pulling back the curtain and sticking out her tongue. She was remembered as being loving and kind.

In her native Italy, Rosa witnessed the complex and controversial unification of the country in 1861, known as the Risorgimento, which translates to "rising again." This movement established Italy as a kingdom under King Victor Emmanuel II, who became its ruler in 1871 when Rome was named the capital of the newly unified nation. However, tensions between Italy's northern and southern regions grew, with traces of this discord still evident today. This situation was somewhat like the American Civil War.

She faced economic hardships, including food shortages. By World War I, her two sons had immigrated to America. Frank enlisted to serve his new country during the war. (At the same time, his future

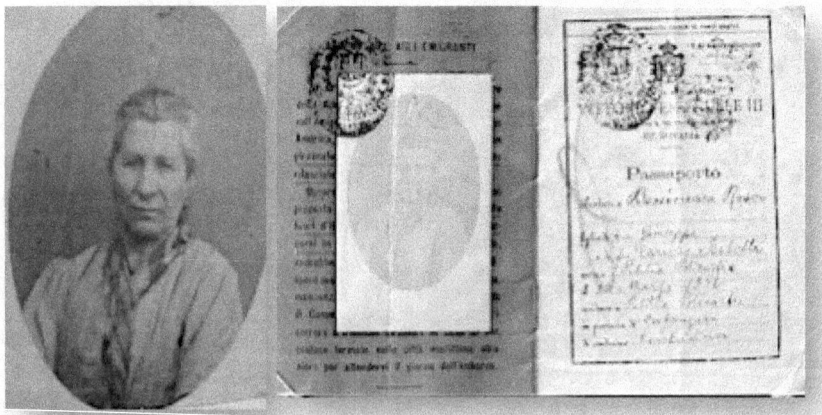

(L) Rosa Benincasa. (R) Rosa's passport. Family archives.

brother-in-law, Giorgio, fought for the Italians in the same conflict. At least they were on the same side!) Her other son, Raffaele, did not serve in WWI, possibly due to a disability in his hand. After leaving Italy with Giorgio and Maria in 1920, Rosa never saw her daughter Isabella again. Nevertheless, all evidence suggests that Rosa had a wonderful life in the United States, surrounded by her loving children and grandchildren. Rosa passed away at the age of eighty-one. The course of a person's life, especially that of an Italian woman of her time, was nothing short of extraordinary.

Life goes on. In 1938 or 1939, Giorgio attended the wedding of Rosalie's stepson, Frank Gelfo. Maria did not go, possibly because Anita was still very young. Rosalie and her husband, John, lived in Detroit, and rumors about a Mafia connection existed. Frank Gelfo's wedding occurred in Rochester, New York, where his new wife's family lived. Visiting Rochester must have sparked Giorgio's desire to live where his business would be more stable and perhaps where the world was a bit more cosmopolitan.

(L) From left: Giorgio Simonetti, Augustine Gelfo (youngest son), bride's parents and bride, groom – Frank Gelfo (middle son), Rosalie Gelfo, John Gelfo, Sam Gelfo (oldest son). Family archives.

Frank Raspa and Catherine welcomed their first child, Ralph Frank Raspa, on February 26, 1927. Their second son, Nick, was born on May 16, 1928. The Raspa family welcomed a third son, Sammy (Salvatore) Joseph Raspa, on December 8, 1929.

Life has a way of reminding you that it is not infinite. Just a couple of years after the loss of Rosa, Catherine Scolish Raspa, wife of Frank and mother of three, died of ovarian cancer on November 25, 1939. She was thirty-two years old. Frank was left without a wife, and the three boys were motherless. Maria and Angelina assisted their brother, Frank, with the boys after Catherine passed away, but they soon grew weary of the task. It wasn't that they didn't love the boys; it was just that they were overwhelmed with their own young families.

Frank Raspa and sons: Ralph, Nick, and Sam.

[L–R] Ralph, Sammy, and Nick Raspa; Mom Catherine in back.

The following year, Maria and Angelina decided that their brother should marry Gemma DeLorenzo. They might have known Gemma's family from the Christopher Columbus Lodge in Fairmont. Gemma was only eighteen, which was more than twenty-five years younger than Frank. Frank was the same age as Gemma's father. Although Frank didn't want to marry Gemma, the Raspa sisters were a formidable influence. Frank and Gemma were married in 1940. She became a loving mother to the boys and an excellent cook. In later years, Frank's oldest son, Ralph, cared for Gemma after Frank passed away.

The daily life of the Raspa/Simonetti clan can only be described as a salt-of-the-earth existence. Giorgio and Maria's brother Frank took the streetcar to Fairmont for their regular visits to the Christopher Columbus Lodge. Maria, Angelina, and Gemma would gather to bake cookies or spearhead other domestic projects. Life seemed to turn on a normal axis day in and day out. We could find no intrigue in this era: no arrest records, no public embarrassments, nothing out of the ordinary.

The 1940 US census listed Giorgio Simonetti, forty-six years old, married to Maria, and living at 390 Satterfield Street with his five children: Thresia, age eighteen; Carmella, seventeen; Ralphine, sixteen; Frank, twelve, and Anetta [*sic*], three. His occupation was listed as Shoe Rebuilder. He worked forty-eight hours per week while owning his shoe shop. His income was recorded as $1,729. Giorgio also owned his house, which was valued at $3,000. He had completed the third grade and was now a naturalized citizen. Additionally, in that census, Frank Raspa was listed as widowed. He was forty-five years old and lived at 238 Clayton Street with his family, and his home was valued at $1,000. His occupation was Theater Manager. His income was stated as $4,000 per year.

The children of the Simonetti/Raspa clan caught a bus to their school in Rivesville, which was about one to one-and-a-half miles away. If they missed the bus, they walked to school, following the railroad tracks along the river into Rivesville. It wasn't unusual to see one of them walking to school with a baked potato in their hands to keep warm during the icy winters, as they lacked adequate cold-weather gear.

High School and First Jobs

In 1940, Thresia graduated from Fairview High School, located about ten miles away from Rivesville. Rivesville High School had burned down and was rebuilt in the late 1930s, so it did not have students who graduated until 1941.

Carmella, circa 1942 or 1943.
Family archives

Carmella was a member of the first girls' basketball team at Rivesville High School (RHS). In 1942, she became the first of the Simonetti siblings to graduate from RHS. Carmella assisted her father, Giorgio, in the shoe shop. She decorated the shop windows with wrapped packages during Christmas, making the store look festive. She also served as Giorgio's bookkeeper. Her siblings contributed to the shop as well. Anita recalls waiting on customers and assisting whenever she could.

(L) Ralphine on RHS basketball team, middle row center.
(R) Ralphine's high school graduation picture. Family archives.

Ralphine also played basketball at RHS. She wanted to be a majorette, but she couldn't afford the baton. Giorgio and Maria couldn't pay for it. Things looked up when Carmella stepped in and bought her a baton. Carmella was likely working at that time and always looked out for her family.

As the siblings grew older, their nicknames for one another became shorter. Thresia was called Tree, Carmella became Car, Ralphine was known as Ralph, Frank was referred to as Hubby or Hub, and Anita went by Neet or Nita.

Giorgio grew increasingly frustrated with Rivesville's economy and its negative impact on his business. By the 1940s, he returned to Buffalo, New York, to visit friends. We have several photos of him on rocks by a large river, but we could only identify the exact spots after hearing stories about his visits to Buffalo. To ensure these pictures were from that trip, we prompted AI to scan them and identify their location. The bot quickly determined that the bridge in the background of our photo was likely the Whirlpool Rapids Bridge in Niagara Falls, which is about twenty-two miles from Buffalo.

Giorgio and unknown acquaintance near Buffalo, New York. Circa early 1940s. Family archives.

Giorgio was undoubtedly scouting for a new place to move his business and family. But the trip was for naught. Maria refused to leave Rivesville because she did not want to leave her family. Giorgio and Maria's life seemed to calm down, but the dogs of war circled once again, and the Simonettis and Raspas, along with the rest of America, were about to confront a test.

The War Years, 1941–1945

When the United States entered the war, the Simonetti siblings, except for Anita, were either in high school or had recently graduated. Since the conscription-age siblings were all women, the Simonetti household did not need to send anyone to war.

Frank was too young to enlist. (He would later serve during the Korean War) He also attended RHS, graduating in 1945. While there, he played the trumpet, participated in a talent show, and, most impressively, painted a detailed mural in the stairwell in the style of Diego Rivera. Sadly, the mural no longer exists.

The onset of the war did not improve Americans' perception of immigrants. The poster shown on the previous page served as a not-so-subtle reminder that the country's language was American (not English, but American). The depiction of the Italian man symbolizes the fascist Mussolini. He proclaims, "We must destroy democracy." This was not a good time to be Italian or to speak Italian in America. We wonder if Giorgio and Maria felt compelled to hide aspects of themselves that represented their old country, Italy, one of the countries (along with Germany and Japan) that the United States was preparing to invade and fight.

In 1942, during the fourth registration, commonly referred to as the "Old Man's Draft," men aged forty-five to sixty-four were required to register for the military. This initiative aimed to collect information on the skills of men who were too old for active duty but could still contribute to the war effort. Men registered by filling out a military draft registration card. The card contained the registrant's name, address, age, date of birth, place of birth, and employer. Over 45 million men between eighteen and sixty-four registered for the draft, although only men aged eighteen to forty-five were drafted. The average age of a US soldier in World War II was twenty-six. Giorgio registered for the Old Man's Draft at age forty-seven. His card is shown below.

Giorgio's WWII military draft registration card. Family archives.

After high school, Thresia enrolled at Fairmont State College, majoring in music with a focus on opera. Like her father, Thresia had a beautiful voice, but she chose not to pursue a music career. She left college and took a job with Westinghouse in Fairmont. During her time at Westinghouse, her beauty once again shone through, and the company used her as a model to promote their products.

Carmella also went to work at the Westinghouse plant in Fairmont, where she proudly supported the war effort as a quality control inspector of radar tubes. Her role was federally funded through the Department of Defense rather than locally. She earned $250 per week, likely double what local Westinghouse employees made and more than most men during peacetime. She was a trailblazer. Carmella was intelligent and competent in everything she undertook. She was also generous, using her income to help her family; there are countless stories of her kindness, not just when her siblings were young, but continuing throughout her life.

Ralphine had been dating Dean Tennant. Although they were the same age, they were in different grades because Ralphine had been held back. In 1943, a year after graduating high school, Dean joined the army and was deployed to Morotai Island in the South Pacific. Ralphine graduated from RHS in 1944 and moved to Cleveland, Ohio, with her sister Thresia in search of new job opportunities.

Thresia and Ralphine lived with a family friend, Lucy Colozermo. They went to Cleveland for work simply because there was work there. While Dean was serving his country in the South Pacific, Ralphine grew restless. During her time in Cleveland, she started seeing a man named Pete. Ralphine told Giorgio that she planned to send Dean a "Dear John" letter and end their relationship; Giorgio, usually an easygoing man, put his foot down. Perhaps he remembered his challenging years in Italy's military and sympathized with a fellow soldier. Giorgio insisted that Ralphine had to wait for Dean to return before making any decisions.

A League of Their Own. Ralphine's softball team in Cleveland. Ralphine is front row, right. Circa 1944. Family archives.

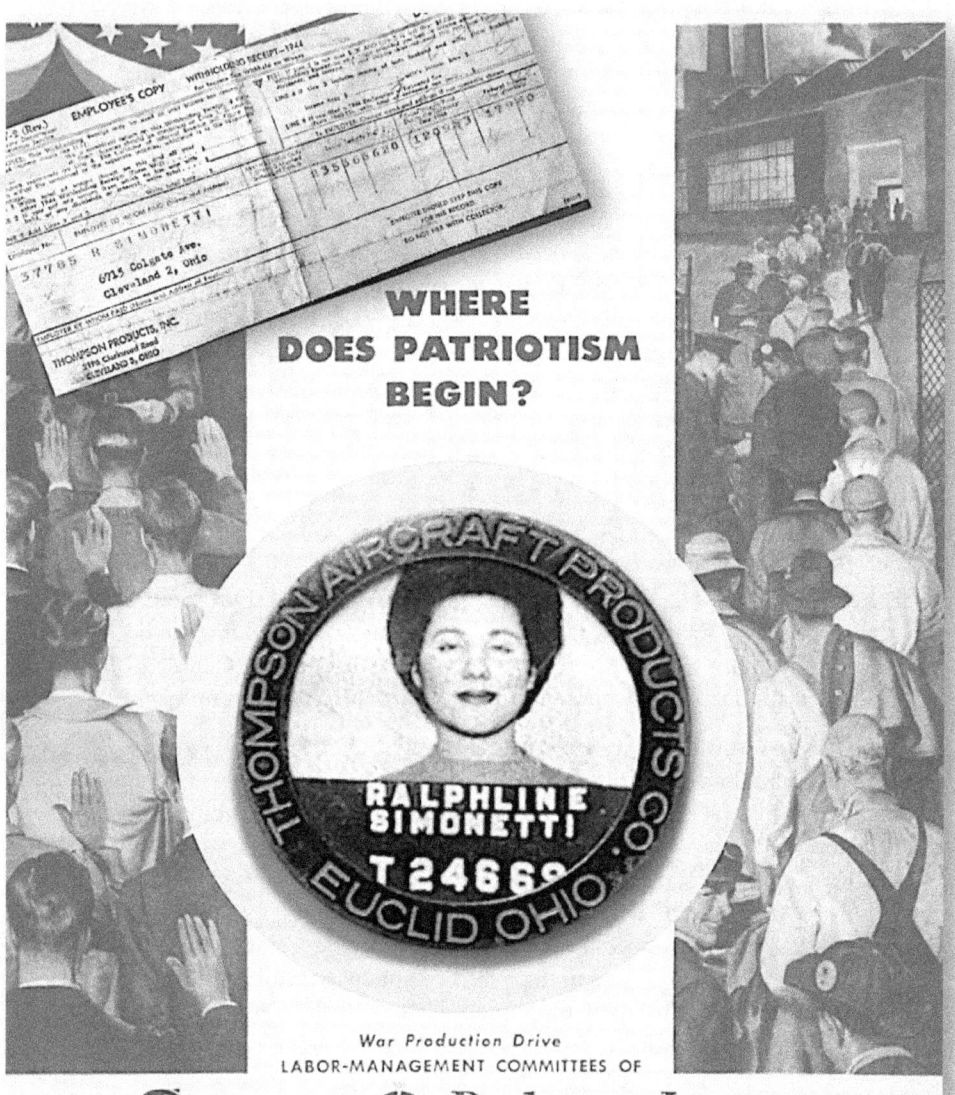

*(Top) Ralphine's W2 from Thompson Products in Cleveland, 1944.
(Bottom) Ralphine's employee badge from Thompson Products, notice her
misspelled first name. (Background) WWII Thompson Products advertisement.
Family archives.*

After high school, Frank didn't want to take over his father's shoe shop. He wanted to leave and follow his dream of becoming an artist. Giorgio then apprenticed his nephew, Sammy Raspa, at his shoe shop. Sammy was one year younger than Frank, and Giorgio hoped that Sammy might want to inherit the shop after his retirement. However, Sammy also showed no interest in continuing Giorgio's legacy.

Death Has No Dominion

And death shall have no dominion.
Dead men naked they shall be one
With the man in the wind and the west moon;
When their bones are picked clean and the clean bones gone,
They shall have stars at elbow and foot;
Though they go mad they shall be sane,
Though they sink through the sea they shall rise again;
Though lovers be lost, love shall not;
And death shall have no dominion.

Dylan Thomas

Welsh poet Dylan Thomas explores the lasting impact of death compared to the meaningful actions that remain in the memories of those who survive us. Death cannot erase the positive deeds accomplished during one's lifetime. It holds no power over the human spirit regarding the enduring legacy of love. The story of Giorgio and Maria is about to take a turn. The *magic* of the era is ending. Though lovers may be lost, love shall not—this sets the stage for Maria and Giorgio's final chapter.

We don't know when Giorgio was diagnosed with terminal stomach cancer, but we believe it happened sometime in 1942. He began seeing a doctor for his cancer in July of that year. The circumstances surrounding his diagnosis are unclear: we don't know how he reacted, how Maria responded, when or how he informed his family, how sick he was, or what specific treatments he underwent. We doubt he shared this information with his mother, who still lived in Italy at ninety-three and longed to see her son. She had last seen him twenty-five years earlier. We believe that before Giorgio became ill, he had planned to return to Italy to visit her and had told her as much, but the war and his terminal cancer diagnosis altered his plans.

While researching this book, we made another serendipitous discovery that offered us a glimpse into the last years of Giorgio's life. Our cousins, Rosemary and Gina Fantasia, Carmella's daughters, were sifting through Carmella's memoirs when they found a newspaper clipping from the *Fairmont Times*. The clipping was old and worn. Undated, we believe it was published around the war's end, in 1945 or 1946. At the top of the article was a picture of Teresa DeLuca, Giorgio's mother, who still lived in Italy. We have only two other photos of her: one with Giorgio's father, Dominico (the one with the little girl holding a doll) and another where Giorgio was dressed as a young girl.

A 93-year-old mother's wish to see her son after nearly a quarter of a century may soon be answered – when the guns of war cease in Europe and George Simonetti, 50, of Rivesville returns to the little village of Catanzara [*sic*] Italy, where his aged mother, Teresa, waits.

For the first time in four years, the Rivesville man has heard from his home across the ocean. His mother, worried about her boy in America, explains in her letter that she had recently seen an American soldier and had asked the Yankee about her kin in this country.

Her questions are numerous, reflecting her existence in a war-torn country. "Have you suffered much from the bombings?" she asks. She explains that they were in danger beginning with the invasion of Tunisia in November 1942. They fled from their homes to the nearest woods about 45 miles distance.

After the Allies took over Tunisia, Sicily, Messina, Reggio and Catanzara [*sic*], and were heading for Salero she and her companions returned to their homes. It was then they discovered that the Germans had raided their homes and taken most of their possessions. "I have lived through many wars," she writes, "and I live on in the hopes of seeing my son just once more."

—Fairmont Times, circa 1945-46.

It's heartbreaking to realize he knew the truth while she did not. The next news she received about her son might well have been about his death. He passed away a year after this article was published. Their reunion song was not meant to be. We know Giorgio was treated at the Cleveland Clinic and may have stayed with his family friend, Lucy Colozemo, with whom Thresia and Ralphine stayed when they worked in Cleveland. True to form, Carmella paid for his treatments at the clinic.

Frank (in his mid-teens), Giorgio, Thresia, and Anita holding Frank's hand. Family archives.

(L) Giorgio and Thresia circa 1944–45 in Cleveland. (R) Giorgio and Ralphine circa 1944–45 in Cleveland. Family archives.

When Dean was discharged from the army in February 1946, he and Ralphine decided to stay together and get married. Ralphine was the first child of Giorgio and Maria to wed. Giorgio, who was super-

stitious, asked Ralphine not to get married on her birthday, July 19, so Dean and Ralphine married in Fairmont, West Virginia on July 18, 1946, officiated by Father James F. Tierney. The service was non-denominational. Dean's father did not attend the wedding because Dean was marrying a Catholic woman. Neither Maria nor Giorgio attended the couple's wedding since it did not occur in the Catholic Church. Giorgio may have also been too ill to attend, even if he wanted to be there for his beloved daughter. Carmella and Anita stayed with their father during the wedding

Ralphine and Dean's wedding picture. Family archives.

ceremony. By this time, Giorgio was in a great deal of pain and he suffered in his bed at 390 Satterfield Street. He passed away at home on August 4, 1946, less than a month after his daughter's wedding.

Anita was nine years old when her father died, around the same age that Maria lost hers. Anita recalls that Giorgio's wake took place at their house and she was sent to a neighbor's, possibly to spare her the pain of seeing him laid out in the living room or perhaps to keep her out of the way. Later, as a professional social worker, she understood that she had never truly grieved for her father.

Giorgio's funeral occurred at the Immaculate Conception Catholic Church in Grantown, West Virginia, a small town near Rivesville. Father James Tierney, from St. Anthony's in Greentown, conducted the Catholic service—the same priest who had married Dean and Ralphine. As Giorgio was laid to rest and the service concluded, the dream that Giorgio and Maria started on another continent, in another era, in what must have felt like another world, came to an end.

The last picture we have of Giorgio, standing on the front steps of 390 Satterfield Street with Dean and Ralphine. He is fifty-two at the time; he looks seventy.

Giorgio's death certificate. 1946. Family archives.

Eventually, Giorgio's shoe shop was dismantled, and all the tools, including Aria, the hammer he had brought from Italy, were sold to the highest bidder. Only songs of Giorgio remained:

One evening, Dean and Ralphine were having dinner at Giorgio and Maria's house when one of Giorgio's customers arrived at the door, interrupting the family meal to ask if he could pick up his shoes from the shop after hours. Without hesitation or any sign of annoyance, Giorgio rose from the dinner table, walked down the street, opened the shoe shop, and handed the customer his shoes, then thanked them for their business.

Was this the song of Giorgio?

When Giorgio returned home from his trip to Buffalo, after he couldn't convince Maria to move, he surprised seven-year-old Anita with a fantastic Scottish kilt and an unusual banana-shaped hat! She proudly wore that outfit around Greentown until it eventually fell apart.

Was this the song of Giorgio?

Once, when Anita was eight or nine and headed to school, a button fell off her sweater. She was distraught, as only young children can be when something small disrupts their world. Maria was busy elsewhere, leaving Anita inconsolable. Giorgio calmed her down and diligently sewed the button back onto her sweater.

Was this the song of Giorgio?

Every Christmas Eve, Giorgio told his children a magical story about how all the world's animals speak on only one day of the year: Christmas Eve. They leaned closer to him in hopes of hearing the talking animals.

Was this, too, the song of Giorgio?

The songs of Giorgio's life, few and serendipitously preserved to be rescored and vocalized a century later, tell the story of a kind, loving, gentle soul who cherished Maria and his family with all his heart. They are the songs of a wounded veteran, a dedicated cobbler, and a cultured man who left behind everything he knew and immigrated to a country that did not welcome him with open arms. Pictures of him at work show the dirty, shoe polish–stained apron he wore and his battered, strong hands. Yet the images of him at leisure convey a song of a bon vivant, impeccably groomed, radiating joy for life. Friends and family surround him in every photo, and an insatiable warmth and love emanate from his presence as if it were vapor swirling above every note of his song.

If Giorgio had songs of life, did life have songs of Giorgio? We must believe there are limits to death's powers. The lasting effects of death cannot erase the enduring memories of love. Death holds no sway over a life filled with love and compassion. What lingers long after death are the vestiges of one's life, notes that have fallen from the original score, collected and vocalized by new generations. Even after death, songs of life endure.

It took Giorgio's loving daughter, Anita, to stage a revival of the songs of Giorgio's life, now arranged from the few remaining notes. We, the authors, have spent over two years seeking the music of a man we never met, whose voice we never heard but whose love endures. Giorgio's song profoundly touched our lives nearly a century after his passing.

* * *

Giorgio, though you are lost, your song is not.

CHAPTER 7: EXTRA★ORDINARY
1946–1975

*Seeds carry life from generation to generation without end. Through the seeds speak
the voices of the ancestors.
Each time we plant a seed we become ancestors for future generations.*

Kenny Ausubel

Our story has no world leaders, movie stars, or once-in-a-generation geniuses. This narrative highlights the ordinary life made possible by hard work, family, and love, even in unbearable harshness. Giorgio and Maria's tale is ordinary. There is immeasurable beauty in the ordinary that takes root and blossoms. There are no Nobel laureates, statues in the town square, or statespersons who saved civilization that come from Giorgio and Maria's story. Instead, there is something more significant: a rediscovery of our ancestors' extraordinary lives.

After Giorgio died, Maria continued living at 390 Satterfield Street. She needed to be strong for her youngest child, Anita. Her older children—Thresia, 25; Carmella, 24; Ralphine, 22; and Frank, 18—must have been grappling with profound grief. In addition to Maria's deep sorrow from losing her beloved, she also faced something many women of that era encountered when their husbands passed away: a loss of income and financial stability. Maria struggled to support herself. Her older daughters provided her with as much financial assistance as they could. Although uncertain, we can speculate that Maria was now forced to handle all the household finances despite her inability to speak and read English. This period must have been somber and daunting for her.

Giorgio did not have life insurance, a pension, or any other support means to leave for Maria. The one wise decision that Giorgio and Maria made was to invest in rental property for income. They owned the upstairs apartment and the shanty behind the house, which Maria could rent.

Maria was only forty-nine when Giorgio passed away. The kind-hearted Maria often allowed relatives to stay in her rental properties without requiring them to pay rent, and few of them thought about paying her. Social Security began in 1935, but initially, businesses like Giorgio's did not contribute, meaning Maria was not eligible for benefits. Maria had no real means to support herself.

Maria kept herself busy. She still had to care for Anita. She cooked, crocheted, sewed, and listened to the radio. She could read and write Italian, while most Italian immigrants in Rivesville could not. When someone wanted to send a letter back home to Italy, they would go to 390 Satterfield and dictate their message to Maria. She would faithfully transcribe their words to send to their relatives in Italy. Similarly, if they wanted to order items, she would place the order at Italian mail-order businesses in the United States for them, including bookstores. She must have had many visitors from the community. We imagine those who needed her translation and writing skills shared a meal with her in her dining room while she helped them with letters, orders, and other matters.

Papino Popolizio and Maria—*The Kindhearted*

In the first nine years after Giorgio died, Maria tried to get by on rental income alone, but there were significant gaps in her income stream. First, Thresia and Charlie moved into her upstairs apartment after they married, but they did not pay rent. Charlie helped around the yard, but that did not pay the bills. Maria was too kindhearted to ask them for money. It did not occur to either of them to offer to pay rent. As time passed, with no prospects for steady financial support, Maria began looking for a husband. Many men had wanted to marry Maria after Giorgio died, but she had turned them all down. Giorgio had set a high standard; he was cultured, kind, loving, family-oriented, and a hard worker. Giorgio left big shoes to fill, no pun intended.

How did Maria meet her second husband? Today, we might say she met him online; however, in the mid-1950s, newspapers acted as the dating apps of that time. Papino Popolizio worked in a bookstore in New York that featured a mail-order catalog for Italian books. Italian immigrants could order these books through newspaper advertisements that Papino's store placed in publications targeted at immigrants. Maria started ordering books, which led to a correspondence between her and Papino. Papino believed Maria was wealthy, which made him eager to move to West Virginia and marry his presumed affluent partner.

At the same time, Maria believed Papino was wealthy because he ran a bookstore in New York. Both were mistaken. While it's uncertain if she genuinely loved him, he seemed suitable husband material. One day, unexpectedly, Papino showed up in Rivesville, bringing pastries from New York to win Maria over. He intended to propose to her right then and there, but this was not to happen, not just yet.

When Maria told her brother Frank that she was planning to marry Papino, he disapproved and questioned who this man was and his intentions. Frank was firmly against it. In a moment of rare frustration, he shouted to Maria in Italian, "Go break your face!" Ouch. Maria Simonetti married her second husband, Joseph "Papino" Popolizio, on May 25, 1955. She became Maria Raspa Simonetti Popolizio. Papino moved into 390 Satterfield. They were happy at first, but as time went on, she came to a significant realization: he was no Giorgio.

When Papino relocated to Rivesville, he began working in Koya's Grocery Store. It is believed that he identified as an avowed communist and unofficially rebranded the grocery as "The Workman's Cooperative." Some viewed Papino as a con artist due to his eccentric behavior. Maria constantly entertained guests at 390 Satterfield. Maria, the kindhearted, always provided food, cookies, and coffee for her visitors. Papino disapproved and was sometimes argumentative with Maria's guests, contrasting starkly with the friendly atmosphere she cultivated. Signs of tension became increasingly evident. Maria disapproved of Papino shaving in the dining room while wearing his undershirt, which she considered a breach of the civilized decorum she valued in her home. Giorgio would never have worn an undershirt around the house!

Tensions mounted, and Maria and Papino soon separated, but for reasons unknown, they never divorced. Papino ended up living above Angelina's former store. He would visit Maria at 390 Satterfield for meals, but eventually, Angelina's store was sold, prompting Papino to move into the shanty behind Maria's house. We don't believe he paid rent, either. As his health declined, Papino's daughter traveled from New York to take him back with her. That was the last time we saw him.

The Raspa Siblings

Maria's three surviving siblings, Angelina, Rosalie, and Frank (Raspa) were growing older. For Maria, the youngest Raspa, seeing them age and die must have been devastating, as it removed the final connections to her Raspa heritage and the early settlers who forged a path for her and Giorgio in America.

Angelina

After WWII, Angelina and her husband, Dominick Gearde, continued to operate the grocery store in Rivesville. They lived in an apartment above the store on Clayton Street.

Angelina's store was a wonder for children. Young eyes quickly darted to the jars of penny candy, sweets, and sodas. Angelina had a large cash register that chimed when she pressed the flat, round keys. A massive scale sat nearby to weigh grocery items. Unlike her sister Rosalie, Angelina was kind and beloved by all. Her two adopted children, Dominick's niece and nephew, were grown by this time.

By the 1950 US census, Angelina and Dominick no longer worked, but they continued living in the Clayton Street apartment. Angelina would have been about sixty-nine years old when Dominick died in 1958. Angelina died at seventy-one in 1960 and is buried at Mount Carmel Cemetery in Fairmont, West Virginia. When Angelina died, Carmella was the executrix of her estate, and her assets were distributed to Raspa's heirs. However, Dominick's niece and nephew were not included in the will. She bequeathed the store to Maria.

Rosalie

Over the years, when Rosalie visited Rivesville, she arrived dressed in furs in her fancy Cadillac. Clearly, she wanted everyone to think she had succeeded in Detroit. After her first husband, John Gelfo, passed away in 1943, Rosalie married Giuseppi "Joseph" Curcuruto, also from Detroit. Maria suspected that Rosalie had a criminal record in Detroit, although the specifics were absent from family lore; her concerns might well have been justified given the Curcurutos' alleged Mafia ties. Following Curcuruto's death in 1965, his children brought Rosalie to Rivesville and left her with Maria. The Curcuruto children disliked Rosalie and were unwilling to care for her, so they dumped her on Maria's doorstep.

Now, in her old age, she lived in the shanty behind Maria's house without income or the means to pay Maria rent. Maria frequently sent her older granddaughters to Rosalie's to wash dishes or tidy up, and she often prepared Rosalie's meals. Like her sisters, Rosalie had diabetes, which severely affected her eyesight. As she got older, her eyesight worsened. She wore thick glasses with red lenses that appeared to glow scarlet when sunlight hit them at the right angle, adding to her imposing look. She had a deep, rough voice, and her demeanor could be quite unnerving. Maria's younger grandchildren found her somewhat scary. Rosalie's relatives described her as "just mean," but Anita saw a different side of Rosalie and got along well with her.

Regardless of others' opinions, Rosalie was Maria's sister, and Maria, the kindhearted, cared for Rosalie until her passing. Rosalie died in 1971 at the age of eighty and was buried at Mount Carmel Cemetery in Fairmont.

Frank

Frank, Maria's brother, was the oldest and only surviving son in the Raspa family. Therefore, in Italian culture, he held the position of patriarch. He took on the responsibility of the entire family and made the necessary family decisions. One of his duties was arranging marriages. Another responsibility of the patriarch was overseeing his mother's care. Frank's mother, Rosa, lived with his family until 1930, when she moved into one of the other apartments above the theater.

When Frank's oldest son, Ralph, was a teenager, he began to manage the theater. He and his brothers gained a reputation for being very knowledgeable about films, which probably greatly benefited Frank and brought him joy in sharing his business with his sons. For effect, Frank would sometimes sit at the dinner table with a knife and fork in hand, banging the utensils on the table and demanding his meal. When he passed away in 1962 at the age of eighty, his son Ralph applied for a grave marker for military veterans. Frank served in the US Army during WWI and is buried in Mount Carmel Cemetery in Fairmont. In his will, written in 1958, Frank left his second wife, Gemma, only three hundred dollars and all the items in their apartment above the theater. However, he requested that Gemma be allowed to live in their apartment or be provided with another home if the theater was sold. The remainder of his estate was to be divided equally among his three sons.

The Simonetti Children

Maria's children were marrying and starting families of their own. Life continued for Maria at 390 Satterfield despite its ups and downs. Her children, now adults, were also experiencing their own twists and turns. Through it all, they stayed very close to each other and Maria.

Cosimo (Charlie) Costantino and Thresia—Queenie

Thresia's beauty was extraordinary, reminiscent of a Hollywood star, and she carried herself with a regal presence. When they were younger, her sisters affectionately called her "Queenie."

When Thresia lived in Cleveland, she fell in love with Buddy Ipswick, a Jewish man. They became engaged, but Buddy's mother did not want her son to marry a non-Jewish woman. Carmella and Ralphine tried to explain to Thresia that the relationship would not work out because Buddy's family was wealthy, and his mother would cut off financial support if he married Thresia. Consequently, he broke up with her because his mother wouldn't permit the marriage.

Later, in 1948, Thresia married Cosimo (Charlie) James Costantino, becoming the second daughter of Giorgio and Maria to get married. Thresia met Charlie during a trip with her parents to visit friends in New Jersey. He swept her off her feet. Thresia fell for him because he was a great dancer, he was good-looking, and he adored her. They met while Charlie was in the army, and Thresia thought he looked so handsome in his uniform. Charlie wore zoot suits with a long chain dangling from his pants and a stylish flat porkpie hat. Although Charlie was from New Jersey, they settled in Rivesville after their marriage, where they lived in Maria's upstairs apartment. After Frank Simonetti left Rivesville, Charlie took over what was left of the shoe shop business, later relocating it to Fairmont. Eventually, Charlie attended jewelers' school, and he and Thresia moved back to New Jersey.

> *Trigger Warning: This story contains themes related to suicide. If you are having thoughts of self-harm or considering suicide, please reach out to someone who can help immediately. Call 911 or the nearest hospital emergency room.*

Charlie and Thresia had three children: Samuel (Sammy), Maria, and George. Sammy A. Costantino, their eldest child, was born on January 30, 1949. Sammy was likely Thresia's favorite. At times, Thresia struggled with her mental health and was unable to care for Sammy, which led him to live with her sister Ralphine and her husband, Dean. When Sammy was about fifteen or sixteen, he was placed in a mental health institution. Concerns were raised about potential mistreatment during his stay. In response, Thresia's sisters Carmella and Ralphine and their husbands pooled their resources to rescue him from the facility. Sammy spent a year living with Maria. He was supposed to return home, but he never did. He graduated from Rivesville High School and attended Fairmont State College, where he faced challenges despite his brilliance. He then served in the Navy for four years and served in the Vietnam War. After his discharge, he returned to Rivesville and married Rosemary F. Sanders. Sammy was a proud United States Navy veteran and a kind, thoughtful young man. Tragically, he died by suicide on November 14, 2011.

Thresia and Charlie welcomed their second child, Maria Lora Costantino, in 1953, and celebrated the birth of their youngest child, George Michael Costantino, on September 4, 1958. George trained as a jeweler, following in the footsteps of his father, who operated the Charles and Son jewelry store. George later married Kathy Ann Roden, and together they had a son, Ryan Charles Costantino, born on July 30, 1988.

> Cosimo (Charlie) Costantino died in 1995.
>
> **Thresia Costantino**, our Queenie, died ten years later, in 2005, lovely and regal to the end.

Nick Fantasia and Carmella—A Force of Nature

Carmella was Giorgio and Maria's second child, and she can only be described as a force of nature. Carmella first met Nick Fantasia through Maria and Maria's best friend, Mary Guzzo. Later, Nick came to Greentown to visit the Simonettis. Carmella was sure he was there to see Ralphine. However, as time would reveal, Nick was not in Greentown to see Ralphine; he was there to see Carmella. Nick and Carmella began dating, and eventually they became engaged. But their first engagement did not last.

Carmella didn't believe Nick was ready to get married. Before marrying Nick, she worked the three-to-eleven shift at Westinghouse as a quality control inspector for radar tubes. Her position was in a government-controlled Westinghouse subsection contracted directly with the US government during WWII, and her pay was two to three times that of other workers. Carmella worked long hours, while in the evenings Nick, who enjoyed dancing, went to the clubs in town.

When Carmella discovered that Nick had been dancing with other women, she told him he wasn't ready to marry. He set out to convince her by showing his loyalty to her. Additionally, realizing that Carmella earned three times what he did, Nick promised her that if she married him, he would take on three jobs to compensate for her quitting hers to stay home and raise their children. On June 18, 1949, Carmella and Nick Fantasia married.

Carmella and Nick's wedding picture. Family archives.

Nick served as a medic in WWII and wanted to attend medical school, so after leaving the Army, he enrolled at West Virginia University. He was pursuing this goal when his father was injured in a coal mine cave-in at the Kingmont mine and ended up with a broken back. Since his father had no benefits or income after the injury, Nick had to transfer to Fairmont State College, where the tuition was more affordable.

Nick graduated from Fairmont State College with a degree in elementary education. When Marion County schools hired him, he and another man became the first Italians to be able to use their real last names at work. Previously, Italian Americans had to anglicize their names to secure employment. Nick accomplished many remarkable things as a school principal and was later elected to the House of Delegates, the state's legislative body. One of his most significant contributions to the Italian American community was establishing *The Italian Hour*, which provided a voice to Italians who faced discrimination in broadcasting.

In 1947, Nick worked at WVVW radio station in Fairmont, West Virginia. Initially, he was not permitted to sell advertising. In 1949, WVVW changed its call sign to WTCS, and Nick began selling advertising, focusing on commercials where the real money was made. He also noticed that many Italian businesses weren't allowed to advertise on the radio, so Nick developed the idea of *The Italian Hour*. The show played Italian music, discussed Italian American culture, and promoted local Italian American companies in a time and place that could be biased against Italian Americans. The show was an avenue for their voices. In 1955, with the assistance of investors, he purchased WTCS. Nick Louis, Carmella and Nick's son, later characterized what could be heard during *The Italian Hour* by imitating his dad's radio voice:

> *We've got Demos Sausage over here. So, if you go there, get a sausage sandwich with hot peppers. And, of course, our friends at Aquarium Lounge are here, and our friends, the Hermacellas, are back there. So please support these folks. They spend a lot of money to come here, and they spend a lot of money to support Italian culture, and the food you eat makes their profit margin. So eat! Mangia!!! Now, we're going to play a little Connie Francis. [Connie Francis sings Volare].*

Nick and Carmella had six children: Georgiana (1950), Rosemary (1951), Nicolena (1954), Gina (1956), Annette (1960), and Nick Louis (1963). Nicolena was her mother's daughter and a force of nature in her own right. She ultimately went to work at the radio station. She was astute and dedicated herself to everything she did. She was the kind of person who demanded her place in the world. At the radio station, she took on a leadership role. Beautiful and intelligent, she did not suffer fools easily.

Then tragedy struck. In 1975, she went on a field trip to a football game at Penn State. At an after-party, she suddenly collapsed and died. Later, Carmella and Nick learned from the autopsy report that she had died from a damaged heart chamber caused by a childhood case of scarlet fever. Nick was never the same; he aged ten years overnight. Carmella, the force of nature, held things together and kept her family moving forward despite her incalculable grief.

Carmella was very influential in her community. She placed great importance on education and family and worked hard to improve the world around her. She served as PTA president, led both Brownie and Girl Scout troops, and was involved with the March of Dimes, the American Heart Association, and the American Cancer Society. Carmella was a founding member of the Kingmont Women's Auxiliary, where she served for decades as treasurer, helping the dedicated group of women transform Kingmont from a former coal camp into a warm, safe, loving community for their children to grow up. For years, Carmella was active with the Marion County Democratic Women and was a proud inductee into the West Virginia Federation of Democratic Women's Hall of Fame.

Carmella was an exceptional cook, having learned from her mother-in-law and Maria. Every Christmas Eve until she passed away, we celebrated the Feast of Seven Fishes, a Catholic tradition, at her home. There was always a steady flow of people coming and going; she loved, fed, and welcomed them all.

No child within her reach ever went hungry or failed to understand that they could stop by her door at any time for a bit of kindness, served with sage advice and guidance. Her other children often recall coming home from school to find a neighborhood child having dinner with them. Carmella knew of neighborhood children who didn't get enough to eat at home and welcomed them to her table. She would bypass the many local grocery stores in Fairmont and drive to Rivesville to give her business to the Italian American merchants from her hometown. Her daughter, Rosemary, sums it up perfectly: "Everything my mother did was to encourage us. She would tell us we can be anything we want to be—you just need a good education and to be kind. She encouraged us to venture out and do things we might not have otherwise done to help others in our community." She knew what she was talking about; she raised attorneys, principals, educators, college professors, a family court judge, a mayor, elected officials, and several entrepreneurs. Carmella was a force of nature. In another era, she would have undoubtedly been the secretary of state or the executive director of UNICEF for the United Nations.

7

> **Nick Fantasia**. At dinner every night, starting in 1975 and continuing for the rest of his life, Nick said grace for Nicolena. He passed away in 2005 as a result of Parkinson's disease.
>
> **Carmella Fantasia**, our force of nature, lived the longest of the Raspa/Simonetti clan, so far. She died on November 20, 2017, after her ninety-fifth birthday. Her force of nature lives on not only in her children, grandchildren, and great-grandchildren but also in the communities she built and the love she engendered.

Dean Tennant and Ralphine—The Life of the Party

We last saw Dean and Ralphine at their wedding, just under a month before Giorgio died. Ralphine must have been heartbroken and devastated by her father's death, which contrasted sharply with what should have been one of the happiest days of her life. After their wedding, Dean hand-built a home for Ralphine on a farm in the countryside, no more than fifteen miles from Rivesville.

Dean attended Fairmont State College, but he never completed his degree because in 1949 he was offered a position as a junior accountant at the Rivesville power plant. Yes, THAT Rivesville power plant, owned by the Monongahela Power Company. In 1953, he became an auditor for the company and transferred to Fairmont. Georgiana and Rosemary, Carmella's oldest daughters, were very close to Ralphine and Dean and would spend weeks at their farm. Today, Georgiana says Ralphine was her favorite aunt, and her favorite memory of Ralphine is her laughter.

Ralphine was always the life of the party and fun to be around. Ralphine and Dean were married for nine years before they had children. They raised three children on the farm: Janet, Nancy, and Linda. In 1963, Dean transferred with Monongahela Power Company to Morgantown, West Virginia, working in a larger city that was home to West Virginia University. Dean and Ralphine knew their children would have more opportunities in a thriving university town. After the move, they welcomed their fourth daughter, Diane.

Although Ralphine was Catholic, she volunteered with the women's group at Drummond Chapel United Methodist Church, the church the rest of her family attended. She participated in a ladies' bowling league and baked thousands of cookies to give away at Christmas. After watching Truman Capote's *A Christmas Memory*, she made delicious homemade holiday fruitcakes. She painted, reupholstered furniture, tapped maple trees to make syrup, and killed a copperhead snake with a hoe to protect her children. She made raucous Halloween costumes. Most impressively, she could start any pull-start lawnmower on the first try. Here is Ralphine in four acts:

Act 1. *When the Simonetti girls were young, Thresia always managed to avoid doing housework because she had to practice her vocal lessons. One day, Carmella and Ralphine were washing the kitchen walls. Thresia made the mistake of standing in front of the mirror beside her hardworking sisters, practicing her scales and teasing her sisters that she did not have to do housework. Ralphine had enough and threw a smelly, dirty rag from the bucket at Thresia. Remember, Ralphine had perfect aim.*

Act II. *One Halloween night after Angelina died, Maria and Papino sat around the big potbelly stove in the center of her store. Ralphine entered, convincingly dressed as an ugly old man. Maria and Papino glanced at each other as this hideous figure walked in just as the store was closing; they had no idea it was Ralphine. He wore a newsboy cap, baggy pants held up by an oversized belt, and a ragged jacket. His face was grotesque, and he had an enormous, crooked Ichabod Crane nose. To Maria and Papino's disgust, he wandered around the store. They were pretty suspicious of him. They knew everyone in Rivesville but had never seen this man. Who was this mysterious, audacious stranger? There was one empty seat beside Maria by the potbelly stove, so the ugly man sat down. Maria was sure he wasn't Italian, so she whispered to Papino in Italian, "What a big nose! What does he want?" The man started inching closer to Maria. As he did, she moved away and asked Papino again in Italian, "What does he want?" This went on for several minutes. Finally, the strange man reached out and swung his arm around Maria, prompting her to get up and run for her life. At last, Ralphine took off her mask, revealing herself. Maria laughed about that for years.*

Act III. *Ralphine never met a stranger. One day, she went to the hospital to visit a friend. Ralphine was on the elevator with her two daughters when a woman got on at the next floor. Ralphine greeted her, saying, "Hello, Birdie," and she asked how she was doing, how her mother was, and if she had made her green beans for dinner the night before. The two continued chatting as if they had known each other for years. When the elevator stopped and Ralphine and her daughters got off, one of them asked Ralphine, "Mom, who was that woman you were talking to?" Ralphine replied, "Oh, that was Birdie. I just met her on the elevator yesterday."*

Act IV. *A friend from out of town visited Ralphine long before GPS was invented. She worried that she wouldn't know which house was Ralphine's, but Ralphine assured her that she would. As her friend turned the corner and drove down Ralphine's street, she noticed that only one house had a bright red dress (Ralphine's favorite color) hanging on the front door.*

Ralphine treated everyone she met with the utmost kindness and total respect. She showed genuine interest in their stories, regardless of who they were, and she never judged anyone, including all the loser boyfriends her four daughters brought home. Okay, not the ones who became husbands, but there were plenty of losers, and Ralphine loved them all. Some of those boyfriends, years later, returned not to see the daughters they dated but to visit Ralphine. She had a gift for making people feel good about themselves because she always inquired about what was happening in their lives. She was the best cook in the world, learning from her mother-in-law and Maria. And to top it all off, she was fun.

Dean also had many great qualities. He was a skilled carpenter who loved building things. Always willing to help others, especially neighbors, he supported Ralphine in all her projects. Ralphine was a fantastic baker who decorated cakes for weddings, birthdays, anniversaries, and other special events. Dean would engineer and construct the structures needed to support her cakes. He could handle any engineering task, no matter who needed it. He possessed what we often call hillbilly ingenuity. Money was tight for Ralphine, Dean, and their four daughters, so they planted a sizable garden that fed their family with the produce they grew.

Dean worked at the Monongahela Power Company in downtown Morgantown. Nearby was a shop where he had his shoes repaired. One day he initiated a conversation with the owner, and luck was on his side. He discovered that the owner had bought his shoemaker hammer and other tools from an estate sale at a shoe shop—Giorgio's shoe shop. Dean loved and respected Giorgio. He knew that this exact hammer was one of the few possessions Giorgio had brought with him when he immigrated some seventy years earlier. After explaining its history, Dean asked the shop owner if he could buy the hammer, but the owner couldn't part with it. In the ensuing years, Dean continued to check in at the shoe store, and when the owner held an estate sale, Dean bought Aria, Giorgio's cobbler's hammer and placed it on a white poster board, surrounded by his distinctive handwriting.

Ralphine Tennant, our life of the party, died in 1995 from multiple myeloma, a painful and deadly cancer of the blood. She did not live to see Giorgio's hammer, Aria, come home.

Dean Tennant passed away in 1999, only one year after purchasing Giorgio's hammer. The hammer is one of only a few artifacts that survive from Giorgio's life.

5/29/98 John DeMignele bought from Mary [Maria, sic*] (Raspa) Simonetti in the late 1940s all of the equipment from George Simonetti's shoe repair shop in Rivesville and moved it to his leather shop beside the Met Theater on High Street in Morgantown. (Some irony here – this hammer may have first been used in a basement shoe repair shop under an opera house in George Simonetti's hometown in Italy around 1919–1920 -and it's final use in a shoe repair shop was beside a theater in the USA). I became acquainted with John DeMignele when working at the Power Company on High Street. He repaired my shoes. After learning that he was the owner of a 'hammer' that Ralphine had used earlier in her life to nail heels on customer shoes in her dad's shop, I offered to buy Mr. DeMignele a new hammer in exchange for 'the hammer.' However Mr. DeMignele was reluctant and he said he didn't think this exact hammer could be bought probably because it was no longer made. He did, however, tell me that I could buy it when he retired. He apparently retired at the end of May 1998. Paul Lattanzi, my coworker at Mon Power, was in the shop early in May 1998. He told Paul about the arrangement, and Paul gave Mr. DeMignele my phone #. Carmella, Nick, and I went to the shop and purchased the hammers and this leather former [not shown] on 5/27/98. L. Dean Tennant.*

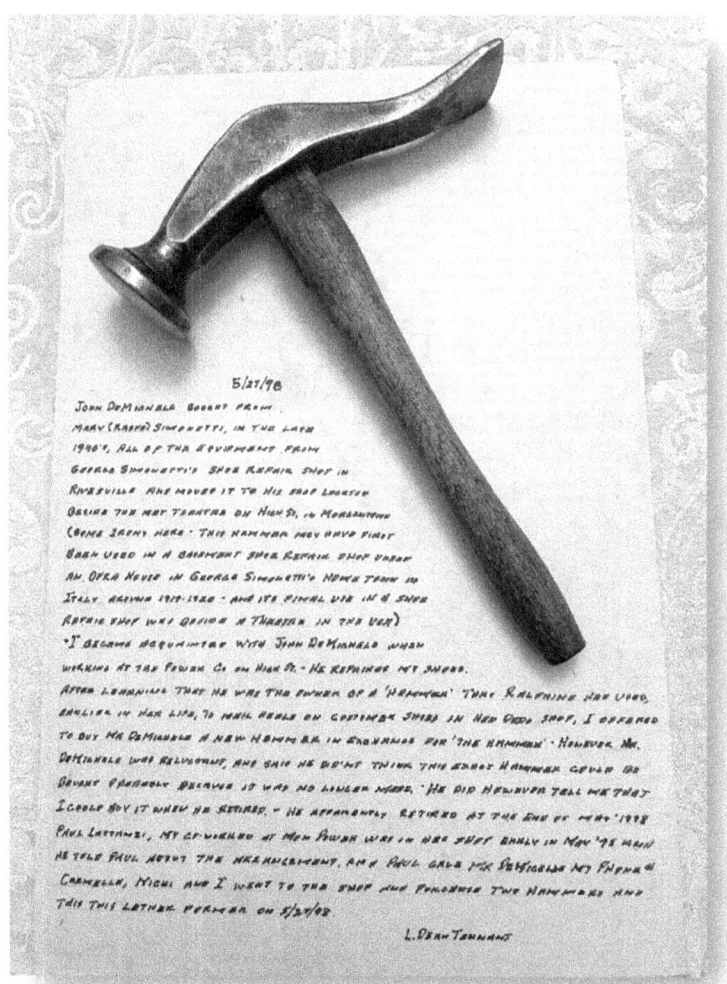

Carol and Frank Simonetti—The Eccentric

After Frank vetoed taking over the shoe shop, he enlisted in the military. Nick Fantasia, Carmella's husband, jumped through hoops to get Frank deferred from military service since he was the sole support for his family, but Frank wanted to enlist anyway. He signed up during the Korean War period on January 16, 1951. As a paratrooper, he was injured when he broke his wrist on a jump, but his family was never notified. For unknown reasons, he disappeared for a time—not AWOL, just incommunicado—and his family thought he was dead. Poor Maria must have been overwhelmed with worry. His eccentricities were starting to emerge. Frank sent his military pay to Maria. Even though she was almost destitute, she saved it all for him when he returned to restart his life. When Frank returned in 1953, Maria, the kindhearted, gave him all the money. He did not expect this. He took the money and purchased a black-and-white Chevy. Then he put Rivesville in his rearview mirror.

An oil painting Frank created in art school. This piece hung above the mantel in Ralphine and Dean's house for decades.

He moved to Akron, Ohio. Toward the end of his life, he regretted not giving Maria the money she had saved. But Maria, the kindhearted, never thought twice about it. He began a well-heeled artist's life in Akron. He always drove fancy red sports cars: Jaguars. He was quite handsome and dressed in stylish clothes, a bon vivant. Remind you of anyone? After relocating to Akron, he enrolled in art school. Frank also worked as a floor supervisor at the Ford plant in Akron. He lived across the street from a popular Italian restaurant where he lunched daily. Over time, he formed a strong friendship with the owners and eventually became a partner in the restaurant. Frank met his wife, Carol, when she dropped out of college just two quarters shy of graduation because she was broke. She walked down the road from Akron to Cuyahoga Falls, stopping at bars and restaurants in search of work.

Carol eventually stopped at a restaurant named Cerillo's. When she got home, she told her sister about a handsome guy she thought was a relative of the restaurant owner because he definitely looked Italian. A few days later, she received a call from Cerillo's Restaurant, and they hired her as a server in the bar.

Carol accepted the position and started working there. She would talk to her sister about the attractive guy who always came to Cerillo's for lunch. Carol mentioned that she would also visit the restaurant when she was not working when she knew Frank was having lunch. After about three months, Frank and Carol began dating. Carol returned to school to become a social worker and an attorney. None of Frank's family attended when Frank and Carol married in Florida, and it was unclear whether Frank had informed them about the wedding. After all, he was the eccentric.

Frank and Carol Simonetti. Date unknown. Family archive.

Carol mentioned that when she first met Maria, she felt nervous and was afraid that Maria would dislike her. Carol was much younger than Frank and had heard the stereotypes about Italian mothers and their sons. Surprisingly, when Maria saw her, she walked right past Frank to reach Carol, threw her arms around her, and said, in her best English, "Now I can die happy because my son is married!"

On one occasion, Carol went to Rivesville and stayed with Maria without Frank. Although Carol couldn't communicate with Maria, she cherished her time there. During her visit, Carol assisted Maria with canning hot peppers in tomato sauce in quart jars. At one point, Carol's skin came into contact with the hot peppers, causing her to develop a nasty rash. Maria took care of her, applying ointments and other home remedies to soothe the rash. This memory is Carol's fondest of Maria because, despite their inability to communicate, Carol felt Maria's love for her. Maria, the kindhearted.

Frank bought a few acres of land with a garage apartment. He sent Carol a card proclaiming that she was now a "land baroness." Frank took great care in personally building an impressive home. He crafted an old-world parquet floor by hand, sanding, finishing, and placing each small piece of wood. He created a stunning spiral metal staircase that he welded himself, and he designed and built a gourmet kitchen. He constructed his driveway, which stretched nearly a quarter of a mile, using pavers he laid by hand. Completing this project took several months. As he neared the finish line at the front of their property, he noticed the county paving the road, which meant his driveway would sit lower than the newly paved surface. True to his nature, he approached the road workers for help, but they seemed unable to assist. Watching in despair as they continued paving toward his driveway, he saw them lower the paving machine just in time, bringing the road down to the level of his driveway. One worker tipped his hat in acknowledgment as they moved on.

Every detail in his home showcased his artistry. He carefully curated his paintings for optimal display. He stated that his goal was for anyone sitting in his house to see something beautiful. Frank earned recognition as an artist who was celebrated for his abstract paintings and metal sculptures. Many of his works remain under Carol's care. Like many talented artists, he possessed an eccentric perfectionism, holding a significant perspective on life's form, medium, color, and technique.

Frank and Carol didn't have children. Later in their marriage, Frank discovered he had fathered a daughter before their union. Lisa reentered Frank's life in her twenties while Frank was in his late fifties. Their relationship was very brief, as he was diagnosed with prostate cancer. Lisa visited her father in the hospital before his passing.

Frank Simonetti, our magnificent eccentric, died in 1991 from complications following a surgery related to prostate cancer. He was sixty-three years old.

Decades later, Carol Simonetti still profoundly mourns his death.

Frank Simonetti

Frank Simonetti paintings, circa 1965.

(c) 2024. Frank and Carol Simonetti. All Rights Reserved.

The picture was taken in Maria's kitchen circa 1962. The occasion was Anita's birthday. Curiously, Maria is not in the picture. Front Row: Nicolena. Second Row: Carmella, Rosemary, Annette, Gina (partially hidden), Janet, and Nancy. Last Row: Ralphine is holding Linda, Anita is holding Roberta, (Anita's daughter) Georgiana, and Gemma. Family archive.

★
7

Maria—Kindhearted to the End

Maria spent decades in her cherished home at 390 Satterfield. Like everyone's life, hers was a series of transitions; first, with her beloved Giorgio and their significant decision to come to America along with her aging mother. They found a way to support themselves and create a home for their growing family. They watched their children use their talents to carve out their unique places in the world. Then Maria lost Giorgio and navigated her adopted homeland through hard times, while some children stayed close and others moved away, blessed with grandchildren and ultimately facing old age.

By the 1970s, Maria was in her early seventies and experiencing declining health. She, like her sisters, had been diagnosed with diabetes. As her condition worsened, Carmella, the force of nature, brought Maria to live with her. By the summer of 1975, Maria was hospitalized in Fairmont for palliative care. Maria's daughters, along with

Carmella's daughters, took turns staying with her in the hospital. After one night, Anita recalled that in the morning, Maria was more concerned about Anita's comfort than her own illness. She encouraged Anita to go home and get some rest. Maria was genuinely kindhearted to the end. On August 4, 1975, Maria passed away from congestive heart failure at the age of seventy-eight.

This Is Water

In David Foster Wallace's famous 2006 commencement address at Kenyon College, he starts:

> *There are these two young fish swimming along, and they happen to meet an older fish swimming the other way, who nods at them and says, "Morning, boys. How's the water?" And the two young fish swim on for a bit, and then eventually, one of them looks over at the other and goes,*
>
> *"What the hell is water?"*

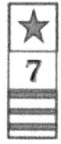

Wallace argues that the point of the fish story is that in the monotony of daily life, the most important realities are often the hardest to see. They become invisible and ordinary. The everyday march of life plays tricks on us, obscuring our understanding of how extraordinary our lives and the people in them truly are. It is only when we slow down and take a closer look that we can see the extraordinary nature of our lives and the people in them.

To some, Giorgio and Maria's story is merely ordinary. It recounts the day-to-day aspects of life, filled with twists and turns and ups and downs. But their journey was as extraordinary as any hero's journey, whether that of a Nobel Laureate or of those who receive a statue in the town square.

Immigrating from one place to another is a universally challenging experience. It's difficult to grasp why individuals take such extraordinary risks, putting everything on the line. For those who chose to come to this country, their journey posed numerous challenges, including obstacles, prejudice, and oppression. Integrating into a new community and culture is as complicated as settling on Mars. Undertaking the immigrant experience requires extraordinary courage, a reality that was true in the past and remains even more relevant today.

"Give us your tired, your poor" was a call to the exhausted and forgotten, but who sent the call? The call was a national ideal, not an invitation from the people already here. Emma Lazarus's poem is about arrival, not the aftermath. Waves of immigrants who came here by choice were fleeing hunger, poverty, and oppression. Upon arrival, they found the golden door cracked open just wide enough to slip through, but then what?

The one thing that made it bearable was the family waiting to welcome you if you were lucky. The actual torch of Lady Liberty is in New York Harbor, but the symbolic torch was somewhere else entirely. It shone from the diasporas throughout the country formed as enclaves of familiarity—a brother/sisterhood in language, food, and customs. In Giorgio and Maria's story, the torch was in the mountains of Rivesville, West Virginia, shining brightly over humble 390 Satterfield Street. The torch lit the way for Giorgio and Maria to envision an extraordinary dream: that future generations would have a modicum of control over their lives and discover better employment, sufficient food, family, an abundance of love, and the freedom to live their best lives.

For those who come next, understand one essential truth: the ordinary can become extraordinary.

* * *

And do one last thing, with gratitude and love

Speak Their Names / Dite i Loro Nomi

CHAPTER 8: BRAVA ANITA!

On Satterfield Street, a young girl with dark skin and scraped knees is carefree as she runs down the hill in front of her family's gray cinder-block home. Her neighbors, concerned about her appearance, invite her into their yard. The older neighbor fumbles in his front pocket, his weathered hand searching for something. A warm smile spreads across his face as he retrieves a coin and holds it up for the little girl to see. Covered in soot from head to toe, her eyes fixated on the shiny coin, a glimmer of curiosity is in her gaze. He leans down and says, "Anita, I will give you this quarter if you go home and wash up." With a radiant smile, she accepts the quarter and scurries home.

Fast-forward twenty years, Anita is standing at the graduation ceremony of Brandeis University in Boston. She proudly places her mortarboard on her head, a symbol of her hard-earned academic success. She has taken a unique path, having graduated from this esteemed institution. As the first and only person in her family to attend college, she is now about to receive her well-deserved PhD. This marks the beginning of her transformative journey from poverty to becoming a beacon of hope for the underprivileged and their advocates. It's an auspicious start for a young woman destined to become a celebrated scholar, teacher, and mentor.

In 1937, Giorgio and Maria had been married for sixteen years. Giorgio was forty-three and Maria was forty. They had four beautiful children. Then, a surprise: Anita was born. By then, her siblings were sixteen, fifteen, thirteen, and nine years older than Anita. One of Anita's fondest memories of her father was when her much older sisters would tease her about being adopted and he would step in to protect her. She must have been the apple of his eye, surprise or not.

Anita created surprises for her family. From a very young age, she enjoyed embarking on adventures around Rivesville—less running away and more like simply breaking free. Giorgio was always searching for her. When she ran away, he would pay local boys to find her, never getting upset; instead, he would calmly take her home.

Anita was only nine years old when her beloved father passed away. At the tender age of eleven, she was struck by rheumatic fever, an illness that left a lasting mark on her life. Instead of obeying the doctor's orders to rest at home, Anita would often sneak out and catch a bus to Bellevue, where she could indulge her passion for skating at the local rink in that neighboring town. However, her risky outings ended abruptly when she accidentally boarded the same bus as her uncle. Yikes! She was quickly caught, bringing her carefree skating adventures to a close.

While recuperating at home, *ahem*, she diligently completed all her homework to advance to the next grade. However, the school overlooked her efforts and chose to hold her back for another year. This wouldn't be the last time academic institutions would slight her, but for now, she focused on graduating. Undeterred, Anita worked hard and skipped a grade in high school, ultimately graduating with her original class. So there!

After graduating from high school, Maria's mother sent her to Lancaster, Pennsylvania, to care for her older sister's children while Thresia underwent surgery. Once her caregiving duties were over, Anita stayed in Lancaster and began working at Educators Mutual Insurance Company at the photocopy desk. Having always dreamed of being a dancer after watching movies with Ann Miller and Leslie Caron, Anita used her hard-earned money to take ballet lessons. Because her legs were strong, her instructor put her "en pointe" immediately. She participated in a recital, sewing her own ballet costume, and continued to dance.

In 1957, while living in Lancaster, she discovered she was expecting a child and later gave birth to a son. During this period, her brothers-in-law Nick Fantasia (married to Carmella) and Dean Tennant (married to Ralphine) proposed a deal. They offered to cover her college tuition if she agreed to give her child up for adoption. She accepted.

At twenty, she returned to Rivesville and began working at a theater in Fairmont while attending Fairmont State College. She started dating Dave Harbert and married him when she was twenty-one. In 1961, their daughter, Roberta, was born. While at Fairmont State, she pursued her dance training and had a second recital. Unfortunately, none of her family members attended. She also took a singing class in college where her male instructor insisted that she sing a song forcefully, which made her uncomfortable. She refused, resulting in him failing her. Anita did not conform just for the sake of it, demonstrating that, even at a young age, she had a strong sense of independence.

In 1962, Anita proudly earned her bachelor's degree in psychology. After graduation, she began working for the Department of Welfare in Fairmont, where she devoted herself to helping others. She then pursued her master's in social work at West Virginia University, where she completed two impactful internships. The first was at the Federal Reformatory for Women in Alderson, West Virginia, where she formed deep connections with some incarcerated African American women. They trusted her and shared their stories, which they did not disclose to other social workers. She realized that one reason for this was that they believed she was a light-skinned African American. Her second internship was at the Veterans Administration hospital in Huntington, West Virginia, where she worked with veterans. In 1966, she completed her master's in social work, marking a significant achievement in her compassionate journey of helping others.

After graduating, she worked at West Virginia University from 1966 to 1970. While there, a friend encouraged her to apply for doctoral studies at Brandeis University. At that time, Brandeis was opening enrollment to students they deemed disadvantaged. Anita remembered that their new definition of "disadvantaged" included poor young people from Appalachia. Anita enrolled and was accepted. Following her divorce from Dave after eleven years of marriage, she and Roberta broke free and headed to Boston. She graduated from Brandeis with a PhD in social work. Her doctoral dissertation in 1974 was titled "The Study of Demographic, Economic, and Political Factors in the Capacity of States to Benefit from Grants," marking the start of her keen understanding of grant writing, an invaluable skill for social workers.

Anita returned to Morgantown and worked at West Virginia University, eventually becoming the acting dean of social work. However, once more, Anita felt slighted. She was not offered the dean's position. In her words, "F**k that!" In 1979, she broke free again, packed her car, and set off for California with Roberta, where she had been offered the prestigious director of social work position at San Diego State University.

Anita has achieved so much in her career; it's truly inspiring. Three significant accomplishments stand out. First, as a faculty member at various institutions, particularly at San Diego State University, she secured over 45 million dollars (in 2024 dollars) in grants and funding. Second, she led the creation of a program for competency-based training for social workers in Southern California, directing a collaboration with the School of Social Work and the county health and human services directors. Third, she has been a member of the advisory committee for the Salvation Army in San Diego since 1998. She has received numerous awards recognizing her outstanding achievements and even has the Anita S. Harbert Outstanding Achievement in Aging award named in her honor at West Virginia University. Anita is retired as a professor emerita and lives in San Diego with her daughter, Roberta, son-in-law, Doug, and grandson, Justin.

In 2004, Anita was contacted by Joe, the son she had to give up for adoption in Lancaster in 1957. After getting to know each other over the phone, Joe flew to California to meet Anita, and they reestablished their relationship. Joe has two sons, making Anita the proud grandmother of three.

Anita has a raucous laugh, lives life to the fullest, and has been a safe harbor for those facing adversity. She has become a true role model for young women and men, not just in her professional life but also for many in her family. She has dedicated her life to supporting the underserved and training social workers to intervene and redirect the course of poverty, abuse, and neglect.

This is truly remarkable, especially considering where she started. Not bad for a young, soot-covered girl from abject poverty, running up Satterfield Street, who broke free to rise to new heights of academic achievement, humanity, and as our family's cherished matriarch, our *Consigliera*.

One of her life goals was to spearhead this book about her parents so that future generations would know something about Giorgio and Maria. Brava, Anita!

CONCLUSION: OUR PILGRIMAGE

As we researched and wrote this book, the word "pilgrimage" resonated in our minds. Initially, it was a weak signal, but as time passed, it grew louder, compelling us to engage with it and explore what it had in store. Why was it buzzing around our thoughts like an incessant gnat?

Religious pilgrimages are journeys undertaken by individuals or groups to sacred sites, often as acts of devotion. For instance, Muslims participate in the Hajj, a pilgrimage to Mecca, Saudi Arabia. Christians often visit Jerusalem, the location of significant events in Jesus Christ's life, or embark on the Camino de Santiago, a famous pilgrimage route in Spain. Hindus travel to the Ganges River and holy cities like Varanasi, while Buddhists journey to Bodh Gaya, where Gautama Buddha is believed to have attained enlightenment.

Our pilgrimage wasn't religious; but it was spiritual. It brought us nearer to the profound meanings of our lives. We were motivated by a personal wish to visit a site of common importance, to search for something we had lost, and to uncover aspects of ourselves. It was, above all, a deeply personal journey.

In literature, personal pilgrimages link protagonists (and readers) to their inner longings: Sal Paradise chasing freedom and authenticity across America in *On the Road*, Christopher McCandless searching for truth in the Alaskan wilderness in *Into the Wild*, and the Joad family traveling west in *The Grapes of Wrath*, hoping to rebuild their lives. Each personal pilgrimage mirrors the human spirit's quest for meaning, belonging, and transformation. Our pilgrimage, at various times, encompassed all these elements. It also raised a deeply personal question: How can we understand and connect with our family members who sacrificed so we could have opportunities for better lives? Giorgio and Maria embarked on their own pilgrimage across an ocean and into the landscape of their new life, aiming to escape hunger and poverty while gaining greater control over their lives and those of their children. Their story reminds us that every step taken to understand their experiences can also lead to a deeper understanding of our own lives.

In some ways, our pilgrimage began in 2016 when Anita, Janet, Nancy, and Linda visited Southern Italy. What we thought was a vacation and a light genealogy visit turned into something entirely different. Setting foot in Calabria gave us an eerie but comforting sensation of returning home. As we followed in Giorgio and Maria's footsteps through Stilo, Petilia Policastro, and Catanzaro, we felt a connection to the land they once walked that could only be explained by shared primordial DNA.

The visit ignited something within us. Upon our return, the spark lay dormant until Anita encouraged us to write a book about our grandparents. We organized, researched, and wrote tirelessly until we held the final product in our hands.

It's January 2025; it has been over two years since we began earnestly working on the book. Everything around us is dead and brown, killed by the extreme winter that envelops us. The grayness is relentless, and even though we know that spring will come, there are moments when we wonder if it's a cruel joke and if we'll be trapped here in winter's chiaroscuro forever.

Seven of us—Janet and her son Michael, Nancy, Linda, Diane and her son Tyler, and our cousin Nick—board our planes to San Diego with manuscripts in hand. We are on a pilgrimage to see Anita and finalize our book. It feels like the invasion of Normandy, albeit on a much smaller scale and with less at stake than saving the world, though no less complicated. We head to Dulles, Columbus, Pittsburgh, and Chicago airports to board planes and start our journeys, hoping that the winter weather won't impede our progress. We gather to discuss the final edits, working through each page meticulously, a painfully tedious but essential process to produce a book that future generations of our family will want to read. As we work, we are also thankful that Anita lives in San Diego, which allows us to embark on a pilgrimage of warmth to the southern Californian sun; not every noble cause in life must include suffering.

This task of writing has transformed us. Giorgio and Maria are mystically present in our lives. Two years ago, we rarely, if ever, thought of them. Now, we find ourselves waking in the middle of the night, consumed by thoughts of them. We try to walk in their shoes to understand why they made certain choices or took a particular path. We have become ancestral trackers, inspired by the trackers of the Old West, searching the landscape for bent branches, footprints, trampled grasses, and broken hooves. We pursue our ancestors with the same fervor until we ultimately discover that we are, in fact, tracking ourselves. What did working on this project mean to us? What is it like to have four sisters with vastly different skills and viewpoints come together to form one voice? How has it changed us? And, most importantly, are we still on speaking terms?

Front L–R. Nancy Tennant, Anita Harbert, Janet Dunn
Back L–R. Diane Rudash. Linda Tennant.

Genealogy has been a hobby for many years. Online research mostly yields facts and documents. However, stories bring family history to life. In writing this book, these stories have allowed me to view my family from a fresh perspective. They were tough and determined, unafraid of change or hard work, with clear goals and dreams.

We are so grateful that Anita initiated this project and took such an active role. As the last surviving member of her family, she recounted stories that were passed down and shared memories from her childhood. What a treasure!

However, some stories shared by my family had a darker side. When I was little, we lived near Rivesville. My father worked weekdays from nine to five, and since we only had one car, errands and shopping took place at the town's stores on Saturdays. The bustling downtown streets were filled with people carrying their lists of essential items like groceries, animal feed, sewing fabric, and banking needs. It was also a time for socializing. Mom always dressed us in cute outfits, and people would stop to chat and tell us how pretty we were. For me, it was a joyful place to be a child, filled with fun memories of good people. Yet, the stories we were told for our book revealed that individuals, sometimes even prominent ones in that town, held prejudices against the Italian community.

Our dad, Dean, a sixth-generation Scottish American, married Ralphine, a second-generation Italian American. While writing this book, we learned that due to their "mixed marriage," they had to endure remarks, slights, and blatant acts of hate and fear from people who were regarded as friends. I was shocked to discover that my parents were targets of such discrimination and that they managed to hide it from their children so completely. They instilled in us values of honesty, integrity, and compassion, never deceit or prejudice.

In those days, men were considered the heads of households, so much of the injustice was likely directed at my father. I viewed him as rigid, uncaring, and old-fashioned. Now I understand that he was angry because there was no solution. Until recently, I didn't realize that he and my mom endured years of hardship and compromise so my sisters and I could become successful, productive adults.

Ralphine and Dean succeeded. Despite all the ugliness, they triumphed. I believe they would be proud of the women their daughters have become, and especially happy that we love being together. I also think Giorgio and Maria would be delighted with our book and very proud of the family that started with them.

—Janet Dunn

"Sisters. Sisters. There were never such devoted sisters." When Irving Berlin penned the opening line of the song "Sisters" for the 1958 film *White Christmas*, he might have been describing the Tennant sisters. The Tennant sisterhood is truly remarkable. For over sixty years, we have remained united through both good times and hardships. When one of us is in need, the other three gather around her and do whatever it takes to help. This support can encompass everything from medical issues to real estate, personal finances, employment, legal matters—you name it. Our commitment extends not only to each sister but also to her family.

While we may not always agree—and, in fact, we often don't—we strive to find common ground where everyone can buy in at some level with shared decisions. This is especially impressive considering how different we are, as highlighted by the unique qualities each of us brought to this book.

Janet is a dedicated researcher with a remarkable knack for uncovering any information she seeks. Her tenacity is well-known, and she has an exceptional memory for dates, names, and details. By the end of the book, she discusses every family member on the family tree as if she knows them personally. Her writing style combines intricate details with a sense of movement, making it engaging to read. Janet isn't afraid to share her opinions and contribute her insights when necessary. I truly appreciated her creativity, which included brilliant ideas and suggestions that enhanced the book's overall quality.

Linda is an exceptional writer. She possesses a remarkable ability to take complex ideas and transform them into something that is both readable and poetic. She shares the Tennant sister trait of determination—being resolute—which has greatly benefited her. Linda puts in the hard work to ensure she is grounded in facts and then passionately advocates for what is right. We all agree that we never want to be on the opposing side of a debate with Linda.

Diane is the extrovert of the group. She enjoys interacting with others. She interviewed over fifteen family members and sorted through more than thirty hours of recordings. With a big heart, she is always willing to help others. Her empathetic nature allowed us to grasp the actions and beliefs of those we wrote about, many of whom can no longer speak for themselves.

Bringing this book to life required a broad range of skills. Watching my sisters' talents come together to create this biography was a joy. Each of them left a distinct imprint on the book. "There were never such devoted sisters."

—Nancy Tennant

Writing this book reminds me of a beautiful musical composition, *Spiegel im Spiegel,* played primarily on the piano and violin. The instrumental scales rise and fall throughout the musical score, creating a sensation of peaceful harmony. I hear the piano as the lovely voice of Giorgio, my grandfather. The violin expresses the transcendent kindness of Maria, my grandmother. Together, both instruments create a perfect marriage. This is my grandparents.

Spiegel im Spiegel is translated as "Mirrors in the Mirror," and writing this book felt like peering into the mirrors of my family. We had family gatherings with aunts, cousins, and friends, sharing and listening to stories about my grandparents. These included tales of my mother, Ralphine, showcasing her mischievous and funny childhood, Aunt Carmella's generosity to the family, Aunt Anita's successful career as the first to attend college, and my grandfather's deep love for opera. As I sat there, I not only listened but also observed their happiness. The mirrors of memories reflected the joy in their lives. And yes, there were mirrors of sadness and flaws, as in every family. But overall, our family stories embodied love, caring, strength, and compassion.

This book began as just a short story, with each sister writing a brief synopsis of a portion of Georgio and Maria's narrative. However, our research raised more questions. When I thought the story was complete, I kept noticing more elements and couldn't stop. The brief outline of just a few pages transformed into a complex tale of my grandparents' lives. They lived in poor and desolate villages in Italy before embarking on a challenging journey to America across the ocean under harsh conditions. It was not an easy story to tell because many unknowns existed. Family members who could have provided answers had already passed away, leaving us with numerous gaps and requiring us to make several assumptions.

One generation reflects onto the next. This is my quest to the reader. Sit in the mirror and ask yourself, who am I, and where did I come from? Understand the harmony of your family and listen to how their musical score was written. I looked into my mirror, heard my grandfather's beautiful voice, and saw my grandmother's transcending kindness. This beautiful composition of two people made me. Wonder what is in your mirror?

—Linda Tennant

When Nancy pitched this idea to my sisters and me, I have to admit I was not enthusiastic. I felt scared and reluctant, not because of the idea itself—I thought it was great—but because I didn't believe I had the skill set to execute it. I've never done anything like this before, and like all unfamiliar endeavors, I wondered if it was achievable.

I would think about it, and it would stress me out. I kept telling myself I needed to start writing. Then we had a family reunion, and I was able to interview and record several family members for my chapter.

I had a relatively easy chapter. The timeframe was after Giorgio's death, so for much of that chapter, I experienced it firsthand. I knew the people I would write about because they were my aunts, uncles, or Nonna. The recordings were invaluable, and I tried to add stories that my mother told me or tales I had heard at holiday gatherings from my aunts.

The recordings and stories I recalled inspired my chapter, which was very exciting. I found myself thinking about it all day at work. I'd remember a story, and when I got home after work, I'd write it down in my chapter.

What's amazing about starting a project like this is that you think you're done, but with every draft, you discover new gems that eventually help create an incredible book.

I never knew what my sisters wrote in their chapters until I picked up our first draft of the book at Staples. I remember when that woman handed me our book, and in the store, I just started to cry. I couldn't believe what I was holding. I remember saying, "This is our book, and I helped write some of it."

When I got home and read the book, I couldn't believe what my sisters and I had accomplished. It was amazing, and I will never be able to repay my sister Nancy for giving me this opportunity, which I would never have taken on my own. I am proud to have honored my Aunt Anita through her legacy and in sharing our family story. What an incredible journey.

—Diane Rudash

*Life is never made unbearable by circumstances
but only by lack of meaning and purpose.*

Viktor Frankl

We all face challenges in life and encounter circumstances that test our limits. Viktor Frankl, the renowned Austrian psychologist and Holocaust survivor, reminded us that between life's circumstances and our responses to them lies a space where we can choose how to react, potentially adding meaning and purpose to our lives. He emphasized that this choice represents our only true freedom.

Perhaps the best we can do is understand our circumstances and live accordingly without addressing the space that invites us to find more meaning or purpose. In essence, this is a perfectly acceptable existence, taking our first step toward a deeper understanding of the ladder of our living heritage. On this first rung, we can enhance our lives by even a scant understanding of the experiences of our present and past family members.

Additionally, we could raise ourselves to the middle rung of our heritage ladder, enriching our lives with an active understanding and empathy for our ancestors and current family members. This might even require some grace and forgiveness. Occupying this middle position on the heritage ladder could instill deeper meaning and purpose into our lives by embracing our living heritage, despite its flaws.

Yet, there might be a higher calling. This calling may urge us to approach life with understanding and empathy for ourselves and others while nurturing aspirations for our present and future families. In doing so, we could ascend to higher rungs on our heritage ladder. Climbing to these higher rungs isn't easy; it requires connection and ongoing grace with those in our lives, along with a deep understanding and empathy for those who came before us. By choosing this third level, we might enrich the dreams of and offer a modicum of meaning and purpose to those who come after us.

We understand, sadly, that some family relationships cannot or should not be repaired. However, we are focusing on the vast majority that can be restored. For instance, we know many individuals who are estranged from their families: brothers and sisters who haven't spoken in years; parents in support groups trying to navigate being cut off from their children's lives; children whose parents' commitment to unconditional parenting ended during their empty nest phase; and colleagues who remain unaware of the ups and downs in their grandparents' lives, much less their parents'. These examples reflect family relationships that could benefit from a more profound living heritage.

With that more profound living heritage, you may uncover ancestors on your family tree who endured unimaginable suffering that often transcended generations. Slavery, hunger, poverty, abuse, and war come to mind—circumstances that deprived ancestors of the chance to pursue dreams of a better life. Their struggle to overcome these hardships is an indelible part of you; it's embedded in your DNA. It has shaped your values and identity even if you are unaware of your family heritage.

If we look to the future, whether we have children, grandchildren, nieces, nephews, or cousins in the next generations, what will these descendants take from our lives? Will they reflect on how we reacted in the space between our circumstances and responses? Equally, what might we pass on to help them discover a space where they can find meaning and purpose?

And what about today? What is the state of our family connections? Can we forgive certain transgressions? Can we establish better boundaries? Can we inquire into our relatives' lives and strive to understand, with empathy, their responses to the circumstances of their lives, even if we disagree? How much effort are we willing to put forth?

Our effort to resurrect our living heritage began with a pilgrimage to Italy, then ultimately turned to telling their story. In this endeavor, we quickly realized that finishing the book was not our true goal; instead, a deeper understanding and connection with family, past and present, and the ability to tell a compelling story that did justice to Giorgio and Maria's lives took over. In constructing the story, new bonds were formed and old ones were reinforced. In Giorgio and Maria's lives, we uncovered two ordinary people whose lives faced their share of circumstances, some extreme, and we learned how they responded. They chose to dream, love, and cherish their extended family and new American community to bring meaning and purpose to their lives.

Before this book, we rarely thought about Giorgio and Maria. Our photos of them were chaotic and scattered across five states. The artifacts they left behind were forgotten or stashed away, mainly without attribution. Their memory was cherished but largely ignored. What has changed is that recovering their story has restored a sense of meaning and purpose to our lives. Their memory is now well cared for, and what their lives represented is now acknowledged and remembered by their descendants. Our act of honoring what their lives meant to us is reflected and felt every time we hear an aria, pass by a shoe shop, hear Italian spoken, or enjoy pizzelles.

* * *

In the cold West Virginia spring of 2025, we returned to the Giorgio and Maria's house on Satterfield Street with Anita as our guide. Our goal was to take a photo on the front steps, just like almost every photo we have of the young Simonetti family. The house is still there, one hundred years later, but it has taken on a ghostly presence. As we approached Satterfield Street, what we saw didn't align with our memories. The block house was covered in an odd, medicinal-hued pink paint and was in severe disrepair. It stood empty, appearing abandoned for many years. The outer door on the upper floor was breached, allowing critters and the elements inside. A fierce dog barked at us from a chain in the backyard. "No Trespassing" signs were posted everywhere.

We lingered on the street, reluctant to risk arrest (though our mug shots would have made a fantastic addition to the book), ultimately deciding against taking the picture. As we got ready to leave, two wary passersby eyed us suspiciously, and rightfully so. Who were we, and what were we doing? Thomas Wolfe was correct: *you can't go home again*. Little did the onlookers realize they were in the presence of royalty; we had Anita Simonetti, the former queen of Greentown, with us.

As we drove away, we realized this is where it all happened, in a time and place that now best exists as part of our living heritage, vacuum-sealed in our shared memory. We have rescued Giorgio's and Maria's names for future generations. Speak Their Names. Their lives mattered because of how they navigated the spaces between the circumstances they faced and their responses with love and perseverance. There, they created purpose and a measure of true freedom for themselves, holding the golden door open for us and future generations to do the same.

FAMILY TREE AND BIOGRAPHIES

Simonetti-Raspa Family Tree   5-Generations, 1921-2024

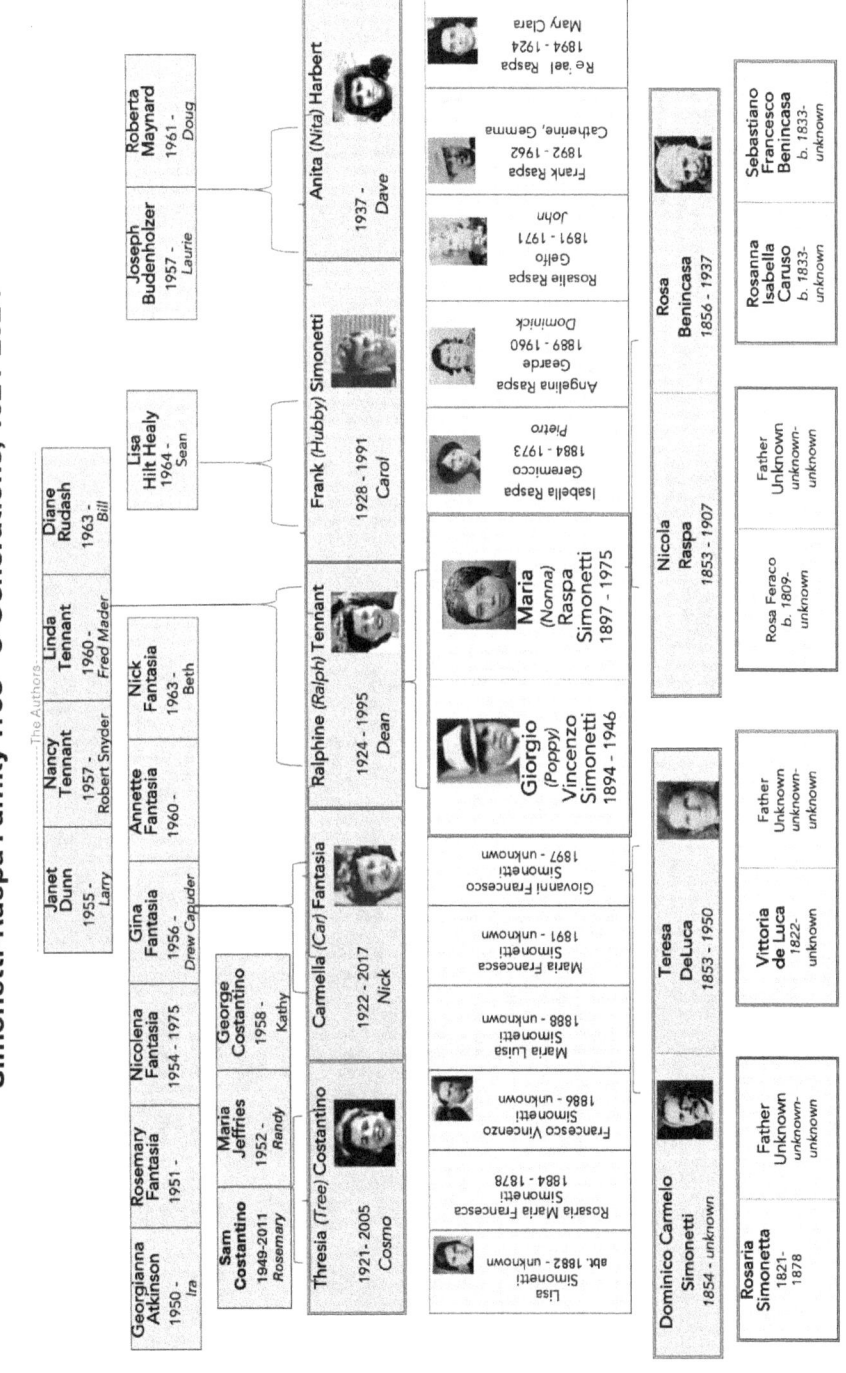

The Authors

| Georgianna Atkinson 1950 - _Ira_ | Rosemary Fantasia 1951 - | Nicolena Fantasia 1954 - 1975 | **Sam Costantino 1949-2011** _Rosemary_ | Maria Jeffries 1952 - _Randy_ | George Costantino 1958 - _Kathy_ | Janet Dunn 1955 - _Larry_ | Nancy Tennant 1957 - _Robert Snyder_ | Linda Tennant 1960 - _Fred Mader_ | Diane Rudash 1963 - _Bill_ | Joseph Budenholzer 1957 - _Laurie_ | Roberta Maynard 1961 - _Doug_ |

Gina Fantasia 1956 - _Drew Capuder_

Annette Fantasia 1960 -

Nick Fantasia 1963 - _Beth_

Lisa Hilt Healy 1964 - _Sean_

Anita (Nita) Harbert 1937 - _Dave_

Thresia (Tree) Costantino 1921 - 2005 _Cosmo_

Carmella (Car) Fantasia 1922 - 2017 _Nick_

Ralphine (Ralph) Tennant 1924 - 1995 _Dean_

Frank (Hubby) Simonetti 1928 - 1991 _Carol_

Lisa Simonetti abt. 1882 - unknown

Rosaria Maria Francesca Simonetti 1884 - 1878

Francesco Vincenzo Simonetti 1886 - unknown

Maria Luisa Simonetti 1888 - unknown

Maria Francesca Simonetti 1891 - unknown

Giovanni Francesco Simonetti 1897 - unknown

Giorgio (Poppy) Vincenzo Simonetti 1894 - 1946

Maria (Nonna) Raspa Simonetti 1897 - 1975

Isabella Raspa Geremicco 1884 - 1973 _Pietro_

Angelina Raspa Gearde 1889 - 1960 _Dominick_

Rosalie Raspa Gello 1891 - 1971 _John_

Frank Raspa 1892 - 1962 _Catherine, Gemma_

Re'ael Raspa 1894 - 1924 _Mary Clara_

Dominico Carmelo Simonetti 1854 - unknown

Teresa DeLuca 1853 - 1950

Nicola Raspa 1853 - 1907

Rosa Benincasa 1856 - 1937

Rosaria Simonetta 1821 - 1878

Father Unknown unknown - unknown

Vittoria de Luca 1822 - unknown

Father Unknown unknown - unknown

Rosa Feraco b. 1809 - unknown

Father Unknown unknown - unknown

Rosanna Isabella Caruso b. 1833 - unknown

Sebastiano Francesco Benincasa b. 1833 - unknown

MARIA RASPA SIMONETTI POPOLIZIO

b. April 13, 1897   **d. July 20, 1975**

Birth Place	Petilia Policastro Italy	*Resting Place*	Mount Carmel Cemetery Fairmont, WV

Maria was the matriarch of the Rivesville, West Virginia, Simonetti family. We believe her father was a bricklayer. She had five siblings: Isabella, Angelina, Rosalie, Frank, and Raffaele. Maria was the sixth child. We believe she and her siblings could all read and write before they left Italy. We have some idea that she and Giorgio were married in Italy before leaving for the United States in 1920, but we don't know. In December 1920, she, Giorgio, and her mother, Rosa Benincasa, immigrated to the United States, arriving in January 1921. Maria and Giorgio were married in Fairmont, West Virginia, on January 20, 1921.

All her siblings, except Isabella, immigrated to the United States, making Maria the last Raspa sibling to arrive. In Rivesville, she and Giorgio were welcomed into a loving and supportive Italian-American diaspora established by her siblings and their families. She became the letter writer for those in the Rivesville community who could not read or write. She and Giorgio had five children: Thresia, Carmella, Ralphine, Frank, and Anita. At the age of forty-nine, she lost her beloved, Giorgio, to cancer after twenty-five years of marriage. Her children gathered around her and supported her, both emotionally and financially. She had no income other than a meager income from the rent of her house on Satterfield Street. After Giorgio died, Maria married Pepino (Joseph) Popolizio in 1955. They were married for twenty-two years. She lived the rest of her life in her Satterfield house. Carmella, who lived close to her, became her financial and family caretaker. Maria lived in the same house until she died in 1975 at age seventy-eight.

GIORGIO VINCENZO SIMONETTI

b. June 8, 1894   **d. August 4, 1946**

Birth Place	Stilo, Italy	*Resting Place*	Mount Carmel Cemetery Fairmont, WV

Giorgio was the patriarch of the Rivesville, West Virginia, Simonetti family. He had six siblings: Lisa, Rosaria, Francesco, Maria Luisa, Maria Francesca, and Giovanni. Giorgio was the fifth child. None of Giorgio's siblings immigrated to the United States. Giorgio was a shoemaker. He worked at the Municipal Theater of Catanzaro, known in our family as the Opera House. There, he made shoes for opera singers. Giorgio was drafted into WWI in 1914 and was discharged in 1919. He was wounded in 1916 at the Battle of Monfalcone, although we do not know what injuries he sustained. He was discharged in 1919. One year later, Giorgio and Maria sailed to America.

When he arrived in Rivesville, he worked only briefly in the coal mines. He then set up his shoe shop, the Rivesville Shoe Hospital. He and Maria led a salt-of-the-earth life. At one point, he had the opportunity to move his shoe shop to Buffalo, New York, but Maria refused to leave Rivesville. He visited Cleveland, Ohio, when his two daughters, Thresia and Ralphine, worked there during WWII. He was instrumental in ensuring that Ralphine waited for Dean to come home from WWII so they could marry. He no doubt knew about the life of a soldier and how terrible it would be to receive a Dear John letter. Sadly, he developed cancer of the lungs and stomach in 1942. He was treated at Cleveland Clinic at one point, paid for, we believe, by his daughter Carmella. By the time Dean and Ralphine married in 1946, he was too sick to attend their wedding. Maria nursed him at their home as he suffered debilitating pain from cancer. He died in 1946 at the age of fifty-two.

ROSA BENINCASA

b. March 16, 1856   **d.** June 13, 1937

Relation
Maria's mother

Birth Place   Petilia Policastro, Italy   *Resting Place*   Mount Carmel Cemetery Fairmont, WV

In Italy, Rosa's occupation was listed as a spinner. She married her first husband, Giuseppe Foreste. They had a son, Dominick, who was the first to emigrate to the United States. Giuseppe died, and Rosa then married a miner, Nicola Raspa. Unfortunately, Nicola died in 1921 when Maria was ten years old. Rosa came with Maria and Giorgio to America in 1921. She was already sixty-three years old when she made the arduous trip.

NO PHOTO AVAILABLE

NICOLA RASPA

b. 1853   **d.** 1907

Relation
Maria's father

Birth Place   Petilia Policastro, Italy   *Resting Place*   unknown

He was a building contractor who built bridges. He was involved in a tragic job site accident. He died shortly thereafter.

TERESA DELUCA

b. December 26, 1852   **d.** June 11, 1950

Relation
Giorgio's mother

Birth Place   unknown Italy   *Resting Place*   unknown Italy

Teresa DeLuca appeared in a newspaper in Fairmont, West Virginia, circa 1944. We are almost sure she did not know she was featured. The story, now in retrospect, is heartbreaking. The story says, "A 93-year-old mother's wish to see her son after nearly a quarter of a century may soon be answered—when the guns of war cease in Europe and George Simonetti, 50, of Rivesville returns to the little village of Catanzaro, Italy, where his aged mother, Terseia [sic] waits. The Rivesville man has heard from his home across the ocean for the first time in four years." The story goes on to say that Teresa was in danger at the beginning of the invasion of Tunisia in November 1942. She fled her home to the nearest woods, about forty-five miles away. After the Allies took over, "She and her companions [it does not say who these companions are, we assume her family] returned to their homes. It was then they discovered that the Germans had raided their homes and taken most of their possessions." She said, "I have lived through many wars, and I lived on in the hopes of seeing my son just once more." Sadly, by the time of this article, Giorgio, her son, was fighting a battle with cancer, and in only two years, he would die. We believe she never got her wish to see her son again. She lived eight more years, six years longer than her son.

DOMINICO CARMELO SIMONETTI

b. 1854   **d.** unknown

Relation
Giorgio's father

Birth Place   Mongiana/Valencia, Italy   *Resting Place*   unknown, Italy

ISABELLA RASPA GEREMINICO

b. 1884	**d.** 1973	**Relation** Maria's sister	**Spouse** Carmen Pietro
Birth Place	Petilia Policastro, Italy	*Resting Place*	unknown Italy

Isabella was the oldest daughter of Rosa Benincasa and Nicola Raspa. She is Rosa's only child who chose to stay in Italy. We don't know where the fare for the steamship journeys to America came from, but it was clear each child had an allotment. Perhaps after Nicola died, they inherited a small amount. Isabella chose to use her money to send her son to school. We uncovered some letters that Isabella and her children wrote to Maria over the years. Isabella's husband died while serving in WWI.

ANGELINA RASPA GEARDE

b. October 9, 1889	**d.** September 26, 1960	**Relation** Maria's sister	**Spouse** Dominick Gerarde
Birth Place	Petilia Policastro, Italy	*Resting Place*	Mount Carmel Cemetery Fairmont, WV

Angelina came to America on the ship S.S. Batavia, which arrived on June 10, 1910. She married Domenico Gerarda (spelling per WWI registration) or Gerarde in about 1904 at the age of fifteen in Italy. There is a family story that her mother-in-law would spank her when she misbehaved. It is unclear if she traveled to America alone. Dominick is not listed on Batavia's manifest. Angeline and Dominick adopted two children. They become the storekeepers in Greentown.

ROSALIA RASPA GELFO

b. 1891	**d.** October 10, 1971	**Relation** Maria's sister	**Spouse** John Gelfo Joseph Curcuruto
Birth Place	Petilia Policastro, Italy	*Resting Place*	Mount Carmel Cemetery Fairmont, WV

Rosalia was the first of the Raspa siblings to come to America. She was sixteen when she traveled alone on the S.S. Algeria, which arrived in New York on July 22, 1907. She is listed as married, and it is noted that her husband paid for her passage. The form states that her husband is in the United States, and his name is Domenico Elia. The details about Rosalia are unclear, but she ended up married to John Gelfo and living in Detroit, Michigan. Perhaps we should say they lived on the murky edge of lawfulness. She became the stepmother of Gelfo's five children. There are family rumors that they had Mafia connections. They ran a store in Detroit. Later in her life, after the death of her second husband, Joseph Curcuruto, her stepchildren brought her to Rivesville and dumped her there because she was so difficult to be around. We heard many stories about her temperament; most we chose not to publish. She lived in the shanty behind Maria's house until she died.

LISA SIMONETTI

b. abt. 1882	d. unknown	Relation	Spouse
		Giorgio's sister	

| Birth Place | Stilo, Italy | Resting Place | Unknown, Italy |

Lisa had a daughter named Maria.

ROSARIA MARIA SIMONETTI

b. 1884	d. 1978	Relation	Spouse
		Giorgio's sister	

| Birth Place | Stilo, Italy | Resting Place | Unknown, Italy |

FRANCESCO VINCENZO SIMONETTI

b. 1886	d. unknown	Relation	Spouse
		Giorgio's brother	

| Birth Place | Stilo, Italy | Resting Place | Unknown, Italy |

Francesco was an architect. Frank Simonetti, Giorgio's son, was named after him. Francesco had a son and, in turn, named him after Giorgio.

MARIA LUISA SIMONETTI

b. 1888	d. unknown	Relation	Spouse
		Giorgio's sister	

| Birth Place | Stilo, Italy | Resting Place | Unknown, Italy |

MARIA FRANCESCA SIMONETTI

b. 1891	d. unknown	Relation	Spouse
		Giorgio's sister	

| Birth Place | Stilo, Italy | Resting Place | Unknown, Italy |

GIOVANNI FRANCESCO SIMONETTI

b. 1897	d. unknown	Relation	Spouse
		Giorgio's brother	

| Birth Place | Stilo, Italy | Resting Place | Unknown, Italy |

Giovanni worked with his brother Francesco.

FRANK RASPA

b. Aug 6, 1892	**d.** April 7, 1962	**Relation** Maria's brother	**Spouses** Catherine, Gemma
Birth Place	Petilia Policastro, Italy	*Resting Place*	Mount Carmel Cemetery Fairmont, WV

Frank and his younger brother Raffaela arrived in the US in 1913 on the S.S. San Giovanni. The manifest listed both brothers as shoemakers. He opened a Grocer's store in Rivesville. He served in WWI. He was married to Catherine and had three sons. Catherine died, and his sisters found him a new wife. Frank was 48, and Gemma, his new wife, was only 18 when they wed.

RAFFAELE RASPA

b. December 18, 1894	**d.** April 28, 1924	**Relation** Maria's brother	**Spouse** Mary Clara
Birth Place	Petilia Policastro, Italy	*Resting Place*	Holy Cross Cemetery Fairmont, WV

Raffaela traveled with his brother, Frank, to America in 1913. The manifest states that he was five feet tall (while other documents state he was five feet five and had twenty-five dollars with him. Later documents mention that Raffaele is missing the first and little fingers on his right hand. Raffaele died at only thirty years old. He was married then and had a son, Nickolas Ralph Raspa. We debated whether to add the picture of his open casket viewing at the cemetery, shocking as it is today. We pixilated his body in the casket. We decided to add it as an archive to show the large Italian-American community that gathered around the Raspas when he died. In the picture, behind his casket, are his sisters, brother, and Giorgio.

Carmella, Thresia, Frank, and Ralphine

THRESIA (TREE) SIMONETTI COSTANTINO

		Relation	Spouse
b. September 23, 1921	**d.** October 6, 2005	daughter	Cosmo (Charlie)
Birth Place	Rivesville, WV	*Resting Place*	Mount Carmel Cemetery Fairmont, WV

Thresia was Maria and George's first child, born September 23, 1921. She graduated from Fairview High School and briefly attended Fairmont State College, where she studied music and voice. Her beauty and looks were stunning and often led her to new opportunities. During World War II, she worked as an office worker at a defense plant in Cleveland, Ohio. While in Ohio, she dated a prominent, rich man and planned to marry him. When the gentleman's mother found out she was not Jewish, she canceled the wedding plans. Thresia then traveled to New York to work on her voice and singing profession. While in New York, she met her future husband, Cosmo "Charles" Constantino. Both returned to West Virginia and married in 1948. They lived in the small apartment above her mother's house. In Rivesville in 1949, she had her first son, Samuel A. Costantino. Sam died on November 17, 2011. In 1952, she had her daughter Maria Lora (Costantino) Jeffries. In 1958, they had their second son, George M. Costantino. The family operated a family jewelry store, first in New Jersey and later in New York. Thresia and Charles eventually moved back to Fairmont, West Virginia. Her husband, Charles, died in 1995. Thresia died on October 6, 2005.

CARMELLA (CAR) DELORIS SIMONETTI FANTASIA

b. November 8, 1922	**d.** November 20, 2017	**Relation** daughter	**Spouse** Nick

Birth Place	Rivesville, WV	*Resting Place*	Mount Carmel Cemetery Fairmont, WV

Carmella was Maria and George's second child, born November 8, 1922. She graduated from Rivesville High School in 1942. During World War II, she worked as a quality control inspector for radar tubes at Westinghouse in Fairmont, West Virginia. She worked there until she married Nicola (Nick) Fantasia on June 18, 1949. They raised six children and were loving parents. Georgianna was born in 1950. Rosemary was born in 1951. Nicolena was born in 1954 and died in 1975 from a heart condition. Gina was born in 1956. Annette was born in 1960, and Nick Louis was born in 1963. Carmella and her husband Nick broke many discrimination barriers for Italians in Fairmont. She was PTA president and volunteered for organizations, including the Girl Scouts, March of Dimes, Heart Association, and American Cancer Society. She was also a founding member of the Kingmont Women's Auxiliary, which transformed the community from a former coal camp into a thriving neighborhood. Her husband Nick was a school principal and also worked in radio broadcasting. He eventually owned his own radio station, WVVW, in Fairmont and broadcasted his famous "Italian Hour" on Sunday afternoons playing Italian music. He was in the State House of Delegates for twenty-six years. Nick died on September 12, 2005, and Carmella died on November 20, 2017.

RALPHINE (RALPH) SIMONETTI TENNANT

b. July 19, 1924	**d.** March 28, 1995	**Relation** daughter	**Spouse** Dean

Birth Place	Rivesville, WV	*Resting Place*	Saint Luke Cemetery Mooresville, WV

Ralphine was Maria and George's third child, born July 19, 1924. She was named after her uncle, Raffaele Frank Raspa, who had died three months before her birth. Her name varies through historical documents, including variations such as Raffelina, Raffalene, Ralphine, and Ralph. She was a band majorette and an excellent ball player on the girls' softball team in high school. Growing up, she was deemed the family's "tomboy." While attending high school, she dated her future husband, Lewis "Dean" Tennant, from McCurdysville, West Virginia. Both Dean and Ralphine graduated from Rivesville High School. At the start of WWII, Dean enlisted in the U.S. Army that same year and was stationed on the island of Morotai. Ralphine moved to Ohio to work at the Thompson Aviation Products Plant (TAPCO) in Euclid outside Cleveland, Ohio. She was the typical "Rosie the Riveter" working on the production floor. Her sister, Thresia, also worked as an office worker at the same plant. After the war ended, Dean and Ralphine married in a small ceremony in Fairmont, West Virginia, on July 18, 1924. Dean attended Fairmont State College to study engineering and briefly worked at the Rivesville Power Station. He eventually started working as an accountant at Monongahela Power Company in Fairmont. They built their own house in McCurdysville, West Virginia, and eventually moved to Morgantown. They had four children. Janet was born in 1955. Nancy was born in 1957. Linda was born 1960, and Diana was born in 1963. Ralphine died on March 28, 1995. Dean died on May 16, 1999.

FRANK (HUBBY) DOMINICK SIMONETTI

b. August 15, 1928	d. October 21, 1991	Relation	Spouse
		son	Carol

Birth Place	Rivesville, WV	Resting Place	Mount Carmel Cemetery Fairmont, WV

Frank was the only son of Maria and George Simonetti. He was born on August 15, 1928, in Rivesville, West Virginia. He graduated from Rivesville High School in 1945. After his father died in 1946, he assumed the operation of the Rivesville Shoe Repair Shop. He joined the U.S. Army from 1951 to 1953, serving as a paratrooper. He then moved to Akron, Ohio, in 1954 and worked in quality control at the Ford Motor Company Stamping Plant in Walton Hills, Ohio. Frank owned an interest in Cirillo's Italian Restaurant in Cuyahoga Falls, Ohio, where he met his future wife, Carol Sue Goff. They married in Broward County, Florida, in July 1968 and returned to Ohio. He was an accomplished painter and sculptor and designed and built his home in Cuyahoga Falls, Ohio. He was also active in cross-country, archery, and skiing, and he competed nationally in marathon races. He has one daughter, Mary Lisa Hilt, from a previous relationship. He died on October 21, 1991, and is buried at the Mount Carmel Cemetery in Fairmont, West Virginia.

ANITA (NITA) SIMONETTI HARBERT

b. March 4, 1937	d.	Relation	Spouse
		daughter	Dave

Birth Place	Rivesville, WV	Resting Place	

Anita is the youngest child of Giorgio and Maria. She was only nine years old when Giorgio died. She moved to Lancaster, Pennsylvania, when she was eighteen. She had a son whom she gave up for adoption. She then moved back to Fairmont, West Virginai, and pursued her undergraduate degree at Fairmont State College. During this time, she married Dave Harbert and had a daughter, Roberta. She received her masters in social work at West Virginia University. She and Dave were divorced after eleven years of marriage. She received her PhD from Brandeis University and became the Director of Social Work at San Diego State University.

Later in her life, her son, Joe, contacted her and they formed a close relationship.

RALPH FRANK RASPA

b. February 26, 1927	d. November 18, 2012	Relation Nephew	Spouse/Partner Edie, Martha
Birth Place	Rivesville, WV	*Resting Place*	Mt. Carmel Cemetery Fairmont, WV

Ralph was the first son of Maria's brother, Frank and his wife Catherine (Scalise) Raspa, born on February 26, 1927. His mother died when he was twelve. His father then married Gemma DeLorenzo, who became a loving mother to Ralph and his two brothers. He graduated from Rivesville High School in 1943. He joined the U.S. Army in 1945. His father and uncle ran the State Theater in Rivesville from 1922 to the late 1950. Before enlisting in the Army, Ralph became the theater manager in 1941 at fourteen years old, making him one of the youngest theater managers in the county. He wrote movie reviews in the National Box Office Magazine and the Motion Picture Herald. He married Edith (Edie) Barth in 1953 and had three children. Daughter Cecilia was born in 1956, son Ralph Michael was born in 1958, and daughter Joni was born in 1961. He was a home builder, building over a thousand homes in West Virginia, Pennsylvania, Maryland, and Kentucky. He retired in 1997 enjoyed time with his partner Martha at his camp near Morgantown and traveling. Ralph died on November 18, 2012.

NICK LOUIS RASPA

b. May 16, 1928	d. February 8, 2024	Relation Nephew	Spouse Helen
Birth Place	Rivesville, WV	*Resting Place*	Mount Carmel Cemetery, Fairmont, WV

Nick was the second son of Frank and Catherine Raspa, and he was born on May 16, 1928. His mother died when he was eleven. His father then married Gemma DeLorenzo, who became a loving mother to Nick and his two brothers. He graduated from Rivesville High School in 1945. He helped his brothers run the Rivesville State Theatre through the 1950s and after his father passed. He attended Fairmont State College in 1949, where he earned a degree in business. At college, he met and married Helen Manzo. They had two children, Kathryn, born in 1951, and Robert, born in 1956. Nick worked for Prudential Insurance in Fairmont, Bellview, and Rivesville for forty-two years. Nick was a fun-loving cousin, always smiling and laughing. He enjoyed his family and friends. Nick died on February 8, 2024.

SALVATORE (SAM) RASPA

b. December 8, 1929	**d.** December 4, 2023	**Relation** Nephew	**Spouse** Delores
Birth Place	Rivesville, West Virginia	*Resting Place*	Mount Carmel Cemetery Fairmont, WV

Sam was the youngest son of Frank and Catherine Raspa, born on December 8, 1929. His mother died when he was ten. His father then married Gemma DeLorenzo, who became a loving mother to Sam and his two brothers. He graduated from Rivesville High School in 1946 and attended Fairmont State College. He helped his brothers run the Rivesville State Theatre through the 1950s and after his father passed. Sam was very active in his high school and college marching bands. Sam married Delores Kozul in 1955. They had one child, Franklin (Frankie Joe), born in 1954. Sam owned his own construction business in Fairmont, building new homes for the Farmers Home Administration. He retired after thirty-three years of service with the U.S. Army Reserve. Sam was another Raspa cousin who loved to dance and have fun. He enjoyed his family and friends. Sam died on December 4, 2023.

NICK RALPH RASPA

b. August 15, 1923	**d.** July 15, 1997	**Relation** Nephew	**Spouse** Juanita
Birth Place	Rivesville, West Virginia	*Resting Place*	Beverly Hills Memorial Gardens in Morgantown, West Virginia

Nicholas (Nick) was the only son of Raffaele Frank Raspa and Mary Clare (Rucci) Raspa. He was born on August 15, 1923, in Rivesville, West Virginia. Nicholas' father, Raffaele, died in April 1924 when he was only nine months old. His mother remarried to Nick Angelo Hando in 1928. During World War II, Nick enlisted in the U.S. Army Air Corps on May 26, 1943. While serving in the Army Air Corps, he was captured by German soldiers and imprisoned in Pomerania, Prussia, and was moved to Wobbelin Bei Ludwigslust. A family handwritten note stated that he was captured at the Battle of the Bulge and was a prisoner of war for about two years. It was noted that his life was probably saved when the U.S. dropped the atomic bomb in 1945, ending World War II. When he returned home, he only weighed ninety-eight pounds. He received the Purple Heart for being wounded by enemy action. Being a prisoner of war, Nick is honored in the Sons of Liberty Museum. He married Juanita Himelrick, and they had one son, Richard Don Raspa. Nick operated the famous Hando's Restaurant on Madison and Adams Street in downtown Fairmont, West Virginia. In 1972, the restaurant was destroyed by fire. The restaurant was not rebuilt in that location. Nick died on July 15, 1997.

SELECTED BIBLIOGRAPHY

Burkett, Connie. "Rivesville, Marion County WV (history)." Marion County WVGenWeb. Accessed September 15, 2024. https://www.wvgw.net/marion/towns/rivesvillehis.html.

"Car Line Is to Be Built to Rivesville, a Town in the County of Marion." *The Daily Telegram*, February 24, 1914, p. 1, col. 2. https://www.newspapers.com/image/354032430/?match=1&terms=Monongahela%20Valley%20Traction%20Company%20.

Fairhead, David, dir. *Mission Control: The Unsung Heroes of Apollo.* 2017.

"Fire Destroys Rivesville Theater in West Virginia." Firehouse (website). August 13, 2004. https://www.firehouse.com/home/news/10509011/fire-destroys-rivesvilletheater-in-west-virginia.

Francis, Henry W. to Harry Hopkins. Report, Clarksburg, West Virginia, November 25, 1934. Franklin D. Roosevelt Library, Hopkins Papers, Box 66. https://web.archive.org/web/20160310055821/http://newdeal.feri.org/texts/440.htm

Good, Colleen S. "Nick Raspa Recalls a Bustling Rivesville in the 1950s." *Times West Virginian.* November 25, 2013. Updated July 27, 2014. https://www.timeswv.com/news/local_news/nick-raspa-recalls-abustling-rivesville-in-the-1950s/article_909328fc-651f-578a-8472-e3a156d1121d.html.

"Interests Mutual." *The West Virginian*, May 13, 1919. Tuesday Evening Edition, p. 6, cols. 1–2. https://www.newspapers.com/image/378528472/?match=1&terms=1916.

"Machinery Does Work of Many Men at Big New Plant." *The West Virginian*, November 24, 1917. Saturday Evening Edition, p. 1, col. 4, and p. 4, col. 6. https://www.newspapers.com/image/465000673/?match=1&terms=meals.

"Marion on the Mon." *Our Stories* (blog). Convention & Visitors Bureau of Marion County, West Virginia, website. June 30, 2020. https://marioncvb.com/blog/marion-on-the-mon/.

"Mayor Richards Gives His Views." *The West Virginian*, June 5, 1922. Mon-day Evening Edition, p. 8, col. 4. https://www.newspapers.com/image/465017779/?match=1&terms=Mayor%20J.%20W.%20Richards.

"Missing Marion County? Make Your Own Pepperoni Rolls at Home!" Convention & Visitors Bureau of Marion County, West Virginia, website. Accessed 2024. https://marioncvb.com/pepperoni-roll.

"New Theater." *The West Virginian*, March 10, 1922. Friday Evening Edition, p. 11, col. 4. https://www.newspapers.com/image/4650017 56/?match=1&terms=New%20Theater.

Ralph Frank Raspa obituary. Domico Funeral Home, Inc., website. Accessed 2024. https://www.domicofh.com/obituary/1828636.

"Rivesville." Convention & Visitors Bureau of Marion County, West Virginia, website. Accessed 2024. https://marioncvb.com/company /rivesville/.

"Rivesville, West Virginia." Wikipedia. Accessed 2024. https://en.wikipedia
.org/wiki/Rivesville,_West_Virginia.

Rotondaro, Vinnie. "Which Italian America?" History. *Current Affairs* (web-site), July 11, 2022. Print edition, March/April 2022. https:// www.currentaffairs.org/news/2022/07/which-italian-america.

Spevock, Frank. *Chimes of Time: A Local History*. Fairmont, WV: Yates Printing, 1981.

————. *A Salute to Morgan Mines*. Montana Mines, WV: F. Spevock, 1979.

"Theater Chains and the Structure of the Industry." WorldHistory.biz. June 24, 2015. https://www.worldhistory.biz/contemporary-history /72764-theater-chains-and-the-structure-of-the-industry.html.

"Voting Today for Greater Rivesville." *The West Virginian*, May 28, 1919. Wednesday Evening Edition, p. 1, col. 1. http://www.newspapers .com/image/464990034/.

Wallace, David Foster. *This Is Water*. New York: Little, Brown, 2009.

THE AUTHORS

Janet Dunn—*1st Daughter*

Janet has had to carry the mantle of the oldest and suffers because she has known us the longest. Janet has fond memories of exploring Greentown as a child, listening to all the adults talk Italian during family get-togethers, and Maria's pizzelles. She is a retired registered nurse and a graduate of Germanna Community College in Locust Grove, Virginia, and Old Dominion University in Norfolk, Virginia. She enjoys baking, sewing, reading, playing music, and researching her family's genealogy. Janet and her husband, Larry, enjoy traveling, being active in their church, and spending time with family. They have two children, Natalie and Michael, their children's spouses, Brandon and Amanda, and three wonderful grandchildren, Camden, Nora Mae, and Aiden.

Nancy Tennant—*2nd Daughter*

Nancy is the middle child and suffers accordingly. She is a graduate of West Virginia University and has a doctorate from George Washington University. She retired as a senior executive at Whirlpool Corporation. She is an adjunct professor at the University of Chicago in the Booth School of Business. She is an author and lap swimmer. Nancy hosts the low-country family compound Moonfish, where all manner of family hijinks ensue. She and Robert are part of a crazy modern family consisting of a swarm of two aunts, three siblings, countless cousins (cleverly disguised as siblings), three nieces, three nephews, three grandnieces, four grandnephews, and three dogs; not necessarily in that order.

7

Linda Tennant—*3rd Daughter*

Linda is the second/middle child—meaning double suffering—and holds engineering and jurisprudence degrees from Fairmont State College, Marshall University, and California University of Pennsylvania. She's married to Fred Mader, who is retired, and they live in West Virginia. She was interested in family history and genealogy from an early age. Linda maintained the family files and photographs to ensure future generations would not forget our ancestors' diverse and rich history. Being an author of this family book has been one of her life-long dreams.

Diane Rudash—*4th Daughter*

Diane is the youngest, with only a mild case of "youngest child" syndrome. She graduated from West Virginia University with an early childhood education degree and a master's emphasis in communications. Diane is married and has two children, Tyler and Danielle Rudash. She changed career direction when she took a position with the Federal Bureau of Investigation (FBI) in Clarksburg, West Virginia. Diane is proud to be a Nonna to her two grandchildren, Rain Christoff and Gabriella Rudash.

ACKNOWLEDGMENTS

Anita acknowledges her neighbor, Mary Juanita Wood, who gave her the idea for this book.

We want to thank all our Simonetti and Raspa cousins (first, second, and beyond), especially those who hosted the Simonetti/Raspa reunion in 2024, who allowed us to interview them *ad nauseam* and provided us with facts, figures, stories, and photos.

We want to thank the Maynards for all their research, and we especially thank Justin for his exceptional photojournalism. We also want to thank our Aunt Carol Simonetti.

We want to give special thanks to our Fantasia cousins, especially Rosemary and Nick, who read an early draft, offered essential edits, and went on several search-and-rescue missions.

It's a miracle that our relatives still respond to our texts and haven't blocked us.

Thanks also to Michael Dunn and Tyler Rudash, who joined our San Diego pilgrimage and enthusiastically encouraged us.

We thank Silvia Baldin for hosting us in Naples in 2016 and helping us with the book's Italian subtitle.

We also thank Harry Davis, who read an early draft and encouraged our storytelling characters.

Thanks to Robert Snyder, who read and proofread the many drafts, and to all our friends and family, who encouraged and helped us at every turn.

Many thanks to our copyeditor and proofreader, Elizabeth Sain.

NAT '24